D1150599

POLITICAL SCANDALS IN THE USA

WITHDRAWN FROM
THE LIBRARY
UNIVERSITY OF
WINCHESTER

KA 0266680 4

BAAS Paperbacks

General Editor: Philip John Davies, Reader in American Studies at De Montfort University

Associate Editor: George McKay, Senior Lecturer in Cultural Studies at the University of Central Lancashire

Published in association with the British Association for American Studies, this exciting series is destined to become an indispensable collection in American Studies. Each volume tackles an important area and is written by an accepted academic expert within the discipline. Books selected for the series are clearly written introductions designed to offer students definitive short surveys of key topics in the field.

Other titles in the series include:

Gender, Ethnicity and Sexuality in Contemporary American Film
Jude Davies and Carol Smith

The United States and European Reconstruction, 1945–1960
John Killick

The American Landscape
Stephen F. Mills

The New Deal
Fiona Venn

Political Scandals in the USA

ROBERT WILLIAMS

KEELEUNIVERSITY**PRESS**

© Robert Williams, 1998

Keele University Press
22 George Square, Edinburgh

Typeset in Monotype Fournier by
Carnegie Publishing, Lancaster, and
printed and bound in Great Britain
by the University Press, Cambridge

A CIP record for this book is available
from the British Library

ISBN 1 85331 189 8

The right of Robert Williams to be identified
as author of this work has been asserted
in accordance with the
Copyright, Designs and Patents Act 1988

KING ALFRED'S COLLEGE
WINCHESTER

320

973.5
/WIL   KA02668804

Contents

Acknowledgements

I am, as always, grateful to the members of the American Politics Group of the Political Studies Association for their indulgence of my long-standing interest in the darker side of American politics. Their comments and criticism have been invaluable. I owe a considerable debt to the Research Committee of the University of Durham for granting me research leave to complete this project, and for the support I have received over a number of years. I would like to thank Philip John Davies for encouraging me to write the book, and my editors, Nicola Carr and Nicola Pike, for their tact, help and efficiency. Last but not least, I would like to record my gratitude to Jean Richardson because, without her support and assistance, the book would not have been completed.

Robert Williams

CHAPTER I

Introduction:
Understanding Political Scandals

Political scandals are a conspicuous feature of American public life. They attract and excite media interest and public attention in ways that few other political events can match. They dominate newspaper head-lines and television news bulletins, and they form part of daily gossip in workplaces, bars, restaurants and homes across the nation. Most Americans have views on what Nixon did during Watergate, what Reagan thought he was doing during the Iran–Contra affair and what Hillary and Bill Clinton may have been doing during Whitewater. It seems that the public are hungry for scandal and the news media are anxious to feed their appetites.

The apparent popularity of political scandals makes them hard for politicians to ignore. A dignified 'no comment' is an inadequate response to the clamour of dozens of journalists and photographers camping outside your house. When the questions come from the FBI, special prosecutors or independent counsels, the need for professional help is evident. Scandals can both disrupt and take over the political agenda of the politicians involved. In some cases it becomes necessary for public officials to resign because they are unable to work while simultaneously responding to criminal allegations. In extreme cases, scandals can paralyze the White House and divert Congress into forms of 'mindless cannibalism'.[1] In modern America, scandals rarely slip quietly away but rather they develop a life and momentum of their own which are hard to extinguish or deflect.

Scandals are not new phenomena in American politics. They are as old as the republic itself. It might be argued that the United States had long enjoyed a reputation as a global leader in political scandal. But to say that the United States has always had scandals is not to concede that contemporary political scandals are necessarily similar to, or comparable with, scandals in earlier periods. Contemporary scandals may be quali-tatively and quantitatively different from past scandals, or the recent spate of scandals may be a symptom of the puritan plague, the drive for reform, which periodically infect the American body politic. Some scandals live in the folk memories of people who have long since forgotten, if they ever knew, what the scandals involved. On occasions it seems almost as if the longevity of scandals is determined less by the actual events or their consequences than by their names. The Teapot Dome scandal of the 1920s[2] is still remembered but the issues involved in the exploitation of oil resources in central Wyoming have never been widely appreciated.

Watergate is a wonderful name for a scandal, and for the next twenty years journalists added the term '-gate' to almost every alleged misdemeanour of public officials. Irangate was briefly a popular term, but the Contra dimension soon rendered it inaccurate. A partial shift has now been made from 'gate' to 'water' because the felicitously named Whitewater development suggests echoes and comparisons with Watergate. But journalists still routinely label other recent embarrassments to the Clinton Administration as 'Troopergate',[3] 'Travelgate'[4] and 'Filegate'.[5] The plethora of scandal allegations is such that scandals lose coherence and identity, and seem to blur into each other. 'Whitewater' has become an umbrella term to cover the original scandal, those subsidiary scandals noted above, as well as the death of Vince Foster, and even Paula Jones's sexual harassment suit against President Clinton.

If scandals have caught the public imagination, they are difficult to understand and explain. There is no obvious correspondence between the degree of controversy generated by scandals and the gravity of the alleged misdeeds. Some of those involved in scandals pay a heavy price: resignation, disgrace and even imprisonment. Others, who seem equally culpable, escape conviction and retire with dignity.

Scandals often involve complex matters where evidence is ambiguous and incomplete. In some cases, teams of lawyers working over an extended period have been unable to establish even a clear chronology of events. If it is difficult to establish the facts, to determine the culpability of individuals and to specify what crimes have been committed, it is not surprising that political responses and public reactions are incoherent and inconsistent.

What is clear is that some political systems are more prone to scandal than others. Where there is a single source of power, where the press is muzzled and where there are no controls or checks on government, it is possible for political leaders to behave with impunity. In such systems, scandals are '*post hoc*' in that only after a revolution or coup are the misdeeds of the former regime exposed to public scrutiny. Until that point, rumours and suspicions remain unconfirmed. If the public are not allowed to know about the behaviour of politicians and officials, if they have no opportunity of voicing their concerns and no means of 'throwing the rascals out', it is hard to see how scandals can arise. Conversely, in a liberal political system with a free press, intense political competition, decentralized political authority and multiple access points, the opportunities and incentives for scandal to flourish are numerous.

If it is not surprising that the United States is especially receptive to allegations of scandal, what is more problematic is to account for the dramatic increase in political scandals since Watergate. Since President Nixon's resignation, we have seen the scandal-induced resignations of attorney generals, national security advisers, cabinet secretaries, the White House chief of staff, the Speaker of the House of Representatives, the chairman of the Ways and Means Committee, as well as senior officials and members of Congress. Sexual harassment scandals in recent years include allegations against President Clinton, Senator Robert Packwood and Supreme Court Justice Clarence Thomas.

It seems that no branch of government or political office is immune to the scandal plague. A roll call of scandals in the years since Watergate is both impressive and depressing: Bert Lance, Carter's Director of the Office of Management and Budget's previous banking record; 'Billy-gate', the lobbying activities of President Carter's wayward brother; Koreagate, congressional lobbying and bribery; Abscam, an FBI 'sting' operation exposing bribery of members of Congress; Vice-Presidential candidate, Geraldine Ferraro's husband's alleged links to organized crime; presidential candidate Senator Gary Hart's sex scandal; the Iran–Contra affair; the Savings and Loan scandal in general and the 'Keating Five' in particular; alleged conflicts of interest involving senior figures in the Reagan administration, including Edwin Meese, Raymond Donovan and Michael Deaver; the Housing and Urban Development department's widespread corruption; President Bush's Chief of Staff, John Sununu's use of public resources for private benefit; the House Banking scandal, use of overdraft facilities; President Clinton's Secretary of Agriculture, Mike Espy, accepting gifts; and, of course, Whitewater and its associated scandals. The list is impressively long but is really quite selective and could have been much longer. It is depressing in that it seems that scandals now embrace almost everyone in public life.

The apparent surge in scandal in the years after Watergate can be explained in a variety of ways. In one view, the primary value of Watergate was to expose how corrupt the American political system is and consequently how trust in politicians should be limited and qualified. The media and the public should be alert and watchful for further evidence of official misbehaviour and should be fearless in exposing it. On this argument, scandal is merely the public tip of the iceberg of corruption. It follows that scandals are proportionate to the amount of corruption in the system, and only when corrupt practices have been reduced or eliminated will the tide of scandal recede. One problem with this argument is that, since Watergate, a variety of measures has been introduced to tackle official corruption. Such measures include campaign finance reform, provisions for financial disclosure, restrictions on post-government employment and new forms of investigations and scrutiny. At the same time, the number of scandals has increased. It may be that all these measures are wholly ineffective but that does not explain why scandals seem to have increased so dramatically.

For those who are convinced that corruption lies at the heart of the scandal problem, the paradox of new reform measures and ever-increasing scandal is not difficult to resolve. From this perspective, American political life has become even more corrupt since Watergate, and this deepening, worsening crisis of corruption brings in its wake a plethora of scandals. The reform measures enacted to date are seen as simply inadequate to the task.

Another way of explaining the surge in scandals is to blame the media. What was once private is now public, and the media are vigilant in their detection and merciless in pursuit of officials who give the slightest hint of misbehaviour or impropriety. As one commentator immoderately observes, 'today's ethics police practice scorched earth warfare of a sort readily recognizable from Vietnam days'.[6]

The opposite strategy is to argue that the increase in scandals, far from signifying any deterioration or crisis in official behaviour, is simply a manifestation of a new determination to find scandals and a reflection of changing sensitivities toward hitherto established patterns of official conduct. Thus the proliferation of scandals is simply a demonstration of the contemporary American talent and appetite for engineering scandals. Instead of scandals acting as the tip of the corruption iceberg, they are simply clouds of water vapour which lack body and substance. From this perspective, scandals are manufactured by those with axes to grind and profits to gain. They distort the realities of American politics by diverting public and media attention away from matters of genuine importance and consequence.

The multiplication of scandals in recent years has helped to create and sustain a deep level of public distrust, suspicion and scepticism of government. Whatever the protestations of public figures and however flimsy and insubstantial the allegations, popular opinion inclines to the maxim that there is no smoke without fire. Political opinion inclines to the view that not only must impropriety be avoided but, more particularly, the appearance of impropriety is crucially damaging to continuance in office. Such attitudes contribute to what Suzanne Garment has called a 'culture of mistrust'[7] in American society. The more scandals there are, the more likely it is that allegations of scandalous behaviour will be made. The more allegations there are, the more there is to report, and the more reporting there is, the more likely it is that public distrust of politicians will grow. The more reporting and analysis of scandals there are, the less chance there is that the ordinary citizen will be able to make sense of what is going on in Washington. In such circumstances, it is understandable that a blanket condemnation of the ethical standards of politicians is likely to be a common reaction to the plethora of scandals.

Any political system that operates in an environment suffused with allegations of scandal and corruption faces great difficulties. When the motives, integrity and honesty of politicians are continuously called into question, the ability of the system to function is placed in jeopardy. Political scandals in the United States have brought down political leaders, discredited and paralyzed entire administrations and influenced the outcome of elections. Yet, despite the evident capacity of scandals to set political agendas, they have received surprisingly little academic attention. Some scandals, notably Watergate, have been extensively discussed but even very recent studies[8] concentrate more on what happened than on examining the causes, consequences and character of political scandals.

What is a political scandal? How do scandals start? Do they follow a similar pattern of events? Do they share institutional and structural characteristics? Why are some scandals more important than others in terms of consequences? Why did Nixon resign and Reagan stay in office? Does Whitewater represent the final victory or the defeat of the scandalmongers? These and other questions are addressed in this volume but it is one of the attractions of the subject that discussions of political scandal are often approached from a range of perspectives and a variety of assumptions. In short, much of the debate about scandals in the United States is the product of partizan, institutional and ideological conflict. It forms part of a struggle not for truth but for political advantage and victory. It is a task for students of scandal to unravel some of the complexities and cut through the propaganda inherent in the subject.

Scandals are events which provoke public concern, indignation or even outrage. A scandal creates, as the *Shorter Oxford Dictionary* puts it, 'a perplexity of conscience occasioned by the conduct of one who is looked up to as an example'. It relates to public expectations of conduct, and what is shocking is less the behaviour in question but the identities of those involved. No one is surprised by pop singers or film stars who sleep around or experiment with drugs but, if a president or a pope engaged in such behaviour, there would be a major scandal. It is thus not the conduct itself but its relation to a public role and the attendant expectations of that role which matter. Scandals involve damage to reputation and conduct which is perceived to disgrace a public office or position in society. For a scandal to occur, there must be public knowledge, and emerging scandals are often dominated by the efforts of public officials to suppress or withhold information. If information can be rationed, the news media managed and the official version of events goes largely unquestioned, the prospects of political survival improve. President Kennedy's numerous affairs did not create scandals because the journalists and editors who knew about them chose not to report them and because the women involved did not 'kiss and tell' until after Kennedy's death. In the case of Marilyn Monroe, some conspiracy theorists contend her 'suicide' allowed a cover up of her relations with President Kennedy and his brother. As Molière wrote, 'to sin in secret is not to sin at all'.

Scandals are defined by political cultures both in the sense that what counts as scandalous obviously varies from place to place but it also varies over time. As attitudes change, behaviour that was once tolerated becomes unacceptable and behaviour that was once seen as deviant becomes conventional. Politicians who enjoy long careers may have to adjust in a timely way to changing standards or find themselves the subjects of scandal. Senator Packwood discovered that behaviour he thought normal and acceptable for twenty years is now judged as harassment and is no longer consistent with continuation in office. But to say that scandal is culturally defined is not an excuse for succumbing to cultural stereotyping. It may be that the British public is more interested in the private sexual conduct of politicians than their French counterparts but this does not preclude concern about the abuse of public office or financial improprieties. In Italy and Japan the notion of scandal seems devalued when what is judged scandalous is also the normal, customary way of attending to political business. In one sense, each country gets the scandals it deserves. As Logue observes, 'Some cultures find sex scandalous, so they are plagued with licentious politicians. Other systems set a premium on money in the election process. Not surprisingly, so do their politicians'.[9]

This book is concerned with political scandals and has nothing to say about the sex scandals involving either presidents or members of Congress. Such scandals may well have political consequences but they are not politically motivated and they do not generally involve corruption or the abuse of power. As Anthony King puts it, 'they are political scandals by accident, not in essence'.[10]

A political scandal involves a departure or lapse from the normative standards that guide behaviour in public office. It may or may not involve unlawful conduct. To assert the connection of an individual with a scandal is not to claim that the individual is culpable in some way but merely that they are perceived by the public to be associated with a particular scandal.

Anthony Barker suggests that scandals are, to an extent, 'defined by their effects rather than their characteristics' [11] [emphasis in original]. But this does not help us gain a clearer understanding of what is meant by a political scandal. Attempts to classify scandals have been fraught with difficulties and, as Barker readily concedes, 'the nub of the problem of studying scandal systematically is the problem of definition'.[12] No two scandals are exactly similar and they occur in different political contexts. The outcomes of scandals can be as difficult to define and classify as the causes and characteristics of scandals. Sometimes there are court decisions or impeachments but many scandals do not result in prosecutions, and prosecutions can be sidetracked by 'national security implications' and by presidential pardons.

Political scandals in the United States tend to involve the use of public office for private benefit and/or the abuse of power in pursuit of policy goals. A large proportion of scandals relates to the cost of elections and the raising of campaign finance. Where individual candidates, rather than centralized political parties, are responsible for generating the substantial sums required to run for office, it is more likely that their relationship to potential and actual contributors will come under scrutiny. Where the regulatory framework and provisions are complex there is more chance of infringing them. In both cases, the likely consequence is more political scandals, and it is certainly the case that many of the scandals involving members of Congress share this common root.

Although every political scandal is different, they all usually involve allegations of violations of the political process and the illegitimate exercise of power. The purpose here is to examine the major American scandals of modern times which highlight such alleged abuses of political processes, procedures and proprieties. In presidential scandals it is important to note that they tend to have two distinct phases. The first phase involves the actual breach or deviation from customary standards and the second phase refers to the subsequent efforts made to conceal or to minimize the breach. Lowi makes a formal distinction between what he terms the substantive scandal and the procedural scandal.[13] The latter constitutes what is popularly known as the 'cover-up' and includes all those forms of political response which serve to conceal, justify, deny, or mitigate the behaviour identified with the substantive scandal. For obvious reasons, the procedural scandal, the cover-up, must follow the substantive scandal but, in terms of their political impact and consequences, the procedural scandal is often the most damaging to the politicians involved. All administrations make mistakes, errors of judgement and experience failures of communication, but a cover-up is much harder to explain and to justify.

Political scandals in Congress pose different problems for the student of scandal. Not only does Congress itself choose what scandals to investigate but it also appoints its own investigators. Members of Congress are, by definition, not executive officers with decision making authority and consequent responsibility. They do not run the government or actually expend government funds. None of the significant congressional scandals of recent years involves allegations of wielding extra-constitutional power or subverting the democratic process. Most often, scandals centre around the improper employment of staff and the links between members and campaign contributors. While members of Congress do not make executive decisions, they are sometimes accused, as in the Keating 5 case,[14] of bringing improper pressure and influence to bear on federal officials to help favoured campaign contributors.

This study aims to improve our understanding of the origins, form and consequences of political scandals in the United States. It is not possible to provide an exhaustive analysis of every political scandal and therefore some criteria for selection have been employed. An obvious starting point was to give attention to scandals that are generally considered the most important. Importance is subjective but intense and extensive media coverage, committees or commissions of inquiry and the appointment of special prosecutors or independent counsel were the most relevant considerations. It was also considered important to see how scandals developed in different time periods and to look at the ways in which changing partisan control of the White House and Congress influenced the evolution of political scandals. Finally, it was thought useful to look at legislative as well as presidential scandals before coming to any general conclusions about political scandals in the United States.

With the above criteria in mind, the selection was made. First and most obviously, the book includes a chapter on Watergate. It offers a convenient starting point for the student of modern American political scandals both because it is often seen as a turning point in American political development and because it is the only political scandal which directly forced the resignation of a president. Watergate is sometimes yoked to the Vietnam war and presented as a defining event that marked the end of an era of optimism, self confidence, and trust in government. The post-Watergate and Vietnam years are, in contrast, sometimes characterized as years of national insecurity, self-criticism and public suspicion, and distrust of government. Whatever the strength of this interpretation, the resignation of President Nixon was a singular event with no obvious comparison. Watergate has variously been given credit or blame for a tide of reform legislation, the weakening of the presidency *vis-à-vis* Congress, the Democratic gains in the mid-term elections of 1974 and the defeat of President Ford in 1976. It is not necessary to accept all these propositions to acknowledge that any account of political scandal in the United States which ignored Watergate would risk being judged eccentric or even perverse. In one sense, Watergate set a standard in scandals and it has influenced the ways in which later scandals have been viewed and handled. This book will indeed argue that Watergate is central to an understanding of the subsequent role and significance of political scandal in contemporary American public life.

The Iran–Contra affair was the most important political scandal of the 1980s and, arguably, was more important than Watergate. While it did not force the resignation of President Reagan, it laid bare the inner workings of the White House and the foreign policy process. It forced the resignation of senior officials and damaged the reputation of President Reagan and other major figures in his administration. The alleged 'privatisation of American foreign policy',[15] the secret sale of arms to a terrorist nation and the diversion of the profits to support the Contra rebels in Nicaragua were dramatic and, to many, shocking revelations.

There are many similarities between the Watergate and Iran–Contra scandals and there is no doubt that the experience of Watergate helped shape both public understanding of Iran–Contra and the ways in which the scandal evolved. It is equally clear that there are profound differences between these two major scandals, and it is not glaringly obvious why they differ so much in terms of the consequences for those centrally involved. These differences highlight the point that the impact of a political scandal often depends more on factors extraneous to the scandal than on the seriousness of the misdeeds themselves or the culpability of particular individuals.

While both Watergate and Iran–Contra involved Republican presidents confronted by an allegedly scandalized Democratic-controlled Congress, Whitewater presents the contrasting picture of a Democrat in the White House being pursued by an outraged Republican majority on Capitol Hill. If the importance of a scandal is measured by longevity and the amount of publicity generated, Whitewater is on a par with Watergate and Iran–Contra. If it is measured by the number and scope of official inquiries and the appointment of independent counsel, Whitewater is still on a par with Watergate and Iran–Contra. But when the political and policy implications are considered, Whitewater seems sadly lacking.

Whitewater may be a spectacular example of a new political phenomenon, the synthetic scandal: a scandal which exists not in the eyes of the average beholder but only in the hearts and minds of the politically motivated accusers. The conservative critics of the Clinton administration reject such a characterization and live in hope that 'a smoking gun' will be found to send the First Lady, Hillary Clinton, to prison and Bill Clinton into political exile and disgrace.

Like Iran–Contra, Whitewater is complex and involves not one scandal but several. Whitewater is, in fact, a classic example of how scandals multiply and diversify, how scandals grow out of each other and spin off in different directions. But when Iran–Contra unravelled, observers felt they had learned something important about the development and implementation of foreign policy in an era of divided government. As Whitewater continues to unravel, we have learned a great deal about the parochial nature of politics in Arkansas, and the Clintons' sensitivity about their personal finances. Yet Whitewater remains the dominant political scandal of the 1990s and deserves close attention.

Given the intense media attention on the White House, it is probably inescapable that presidential scandals receive more publicity than their congressional counterparts. Congressional scandals lack dramatic impact and, while members of Congress are keen to be seen investigating presidential scandals, preferably on prime-time television, their own ethics committees in the House and Senate prefer to conduct their business behind closed doors. Institutional and partisan rivalries no doubt account for much of the difference in approach but members of Congress are apprehensive about investigating one another, and assignments to the ethics committees are not seen as legislative prizes.

Before Watergate, Congress still had some of the qualities of a club in which members' behaviour had to be truly egregious to warrant publicity and firm disciplinary action. There were exceptions to this rule, such as the scandals involving Adam Clayton Powell in the 1960s,[16] but, as a high-profile black in an overwhelmingly white club, he was always treated as an outsider. Powell himself frequently claimed that his behaviour was no more scandalous than that of many other members of Congress. In his view, it was his race not his behaviour which created the scandal.

Since Watergate there have been major changes in Congress. In the 1970s, committee chairmen were shaken by a challenge to the seniority system facilitated in part by the large freshman Democratic intake in 1974. In the 1980s Republican leaders in the House and Senate struggled to resist the Democratic majority over the Iran–Contra scandal. In part, this partisan friction contributed to a decline in comity in Congress and increasingly effective attacks by Republicans on the Democratic leadership in Congress. As Chapter 5, on Congress, shows, political scandal was a major weapon in the armoury of the Republic minority. In the 1980s and 1990s, congressional leaders have been driven from office by scandal allegations, and this evolution in congressional attitudes and behaviour is clearly important in understanding the role of political scandal in American politics.

Whether a political scandal is presidential or congressional in character, there are similar, if not identical, phases in their evolution. The dance of scandal has familiar steps: allegation, denial, exposure, inquiry, cover-up, fresh allegations, further enquiries and sometimes even a conclusion. Questions are posed and, if unanswered, they heighten the sense of scandal. If answered the answers provide new facts to check and rebut. The search goes deeper and backward in time to look at the accused's record. Vice-President Spiro Agnew resigned not for crimes committed in office but for his conduct as a state official and later as Governor of Maryland. Much of the Whitewater scandal is concerned with events in Arkansas which occurred fifteen years before Clinton reached the White House. Like tree roots, scandal-hunters burrow beneath the façade of public office to disturb long-buried skeletons.

The purpose of this book is to look behind the facade of political scandals in the United States in order to understand how they begin, how they develop and how they influence the form and character of the political process. However distasteful it is for those embroiled in political scandal, they are a conspicuous and inescapable part of contemporary American politics. The dogs of scandal are always hungry and however many bones are tossed to them, their appetite for their quarry remains undiminished. Political scandals are here to stay and it is essential that students of American politics understand their nature and significance.

Notes

1. Speaker Jim Wright's resignation speech, 31 May 1989 as quoted in J. Dumbrell, 'Corruption and ethics codes in Congress', *Corruption and Reform*, vol. 6, No. 2, 1991, p. 147.
2. J. Leonard Bates, *The Origins of Teapot Dome: Progressives, Parties and Petroleum, 1909–1921* (Urbana: University of Illinois Press, 1963).
3. 'Troopergate' refers to the allegations made by a group of Arkansas state troopers about Clinton's liaisons with women while he was Governor of Arkansas.
4. 'Travelgate' refers to the firing of White House travel office employees and the First Lady's alleged involvement.
5. 'Filegate' refers to White House scrutiny of confidential FBI background files of Republican employees in the Bush administration.
6. Suzanne Garment, *Scandal: the Crisis of Mistrust in American Politics* (New York: Times Books, Random House, 1991), p. 8.
7. Garment, p. 2.
8. Fred Emery, *Watergate: The Corruption and Fall of Richard Nixon* (London: Jonathan Cape, 1994).
9. John Logue in A. S. Markovits and M. Silverstein (eds), *The Politics of Scandal: Power and Process in Liberal Democracies* (New York: Holmes and Meier, 1988), p. 264.

10. Anthony King, 'Sex, Money and Power: Political Scandals in Great Britain and the United States', *Essex Papers in Politics and Government*, No. 14, 1984, p. 20.
11. Anthony Barker, 'The Upturned Stone – Political Scandals in Twenty Democracies and their Investigation Processes', *Essex Papers in Politics and Government*, No. 90, 1992, p. 16.
12. Barker, p. 28.
13. Theodore J. Lowi in Markovits and Silverstein, p. viii.
14. The Keating Five were Senators Alan Cranston, Dennis DeConcini, John Glenn, Donald Riegle (Democrats) and Senator John McCain (Republican).
15. Senator Daniel Inouye quoted in M. Shaw (ed.), *Roosevelt to Reagan: The Development of the Modern Presidency* (London: C. Hurst and Co., 1987), p. 309.
16. Robert S. Getz, *Congressional Ethics: The Conflict of Interest Issue* (Princeton, New Jersey: D. Van Nostrand Inc., 1966), pp. 104–11.

CHAPTER 2

Watergate

The Watergate scandal is no longer a national obsession but it is difficult to underestimate its resonance with those who lived through it. A military aide to President Gerald Ford observed: 'We're all Watergate junkies. Some of us are mainlining, some are sniffing, some are lacing it with something else, but all of us are addicted. This will go on and on unless someone steps in and says that we, as a nation, must go cold turkey. Otherwise, we'll die of an overdose.' [1] The 'someone' who did was President Ford and his reward was to see his approval rating fall 22 per cent in a month in response to his pardon of Nixon.

President Ford's announcement of a 'full, free and absolute pardon' to Richard Nixon in September 1974 brought to a formal end a political scandal whose origins are to be found in the political atmosphere of the White House early in Nixon's first term. This chapter will give a brief account of the events which make up the scandal before discussing its causes, character and consequences. As with other scandals, differing perspectives produce different accounts and interpretations. The importance of the Watergate scandal is to be found not just in the tumultuous events of 1972–4 but in the extent to which political scandals since that period have, to a greater or lesser extent, been viewed through Watergate-tinted spectacles.

The origins of Watergate are to be found in an interagency task force which was established in 1970 to consider the threat posed by subversive groups and how to tackle that threat. A report (the Huston Plan) [2] was prepared for President Nixon, but FBI Director, J. Edgar Hoover, voiced strong objections. In a separate memorandum, Huston encouraged the use of 'surreptitious entry' because, despite its illegality and dangers, 'it is also the most fruitful tool and can produce the type of intelligence which cannot be obtained in any other fashion'.[3] The ostensible targets of such activities were radical protest groups like the Black Panthers and the Weathermen.

But Hoover's intransigence and refusal to co-operate with other agencies meant that the Huston plan had to be abandoned. While informal and *ad hoc* surveillance of 'enemies' of the administration continued, the event that crystallized White House strategy was the leaking of the so-called Pentagon Papers,[4] publication of which began in the *New York Times* on 13 June 1971. The publication of top secret material inflamed the Nixon White House and the government sought an injunction to prevent publication. On 30 June 1971, the Supreme Court rejected by 6–3 the government's case. The legal case centred on the issue of prior restraint on publication and did not protect the 'leakers', in particular, Dr Daniel Ellsberg, from possible prosecution.

Nixon's view was that it was imperative to 'get' Ellsberg by any means necessary, not merely to discourage others but to convince foreign governments that the United States could protect its secrets. The criminal justice system was swiftly cranked into operation and Ellsberg was indicted on charges of unauthorized possession of secret material and theft of government property. FBI wiretap reports on Ellsberg were removed to the White House. In July 1971, the decision was taken to form a White House Special Investigation Unit otherwise known as 'the Plumbers' because they took action on leaks. In September 1971, the Plumbers orchestrated the burglary of Dr Fielding, Ellsberg's psychiatrist apparently on the authority of John Erlichman, chief domestic policy adviser to President Nixon.[5]

With the approach of the 1972 presidential election, attention was increasingly given to gathering political intelligence on the Democratic Party and its leading candidates. Some of the Plumbers had moved over to the Committee to Re-elect the President (CRP). The new security co-ordinator at CRP was a former CIA man, James McCord, and he was asked to join an operation to bug the Democratic Party headquarters at the Watergate building in Washington. It proved an unfortunate choice in that McCord could subsequently be directly linked to the Nixon re-election campaign.

In the early hours of 17 June 1972, a private security guard, Frank Wills, discovered that doors in the Watergate building had been taped to stay unlocked. He called the police and the five Watergate burglars were arrested. E. Howard Hunt and G. Gordon Liddy, who had planned the burglaries, organized lawyers to try to get the burglars released on bail. Liddy also contacted Jeb Magruder, deputy director of CRP, to tell him of McCord's arrest. In turn, John Mitchell, former Attorney General and Director of CRP, was informed and, on behalf of Mitchell, Liddy approached the new Attorney General, Richard Kleindienst, and asked him to intervene and get McCord out of custody before his identity was discovered. Kleindienst declined to co-operate but his refusal was based less on legal grounds and more on the probable political repercussions for President Nixon.

Documents left in hotel rooms opposite the Watergate complex directly linked two of the burglars to Hunt and, within a few hours, the FBI had established that Hunt was a White House consultant. The burglary at the Watergate had been linked to the White House before the investigators appreciated it was also linked to Nixon's campaign organization. The news soon reached Nixon's top two aides, Haldeman and Erlichman, and the latter realized that the Watergate burglaries were the work of the same group he had used for the burglary of Ellsberg's psychiatrist.

When McCord was in court that afternoon, he was recognized by police officers as an employee at CRP, and the FBI realized that this was a case with unknown but profound political implications. When asked his occupation, McCord answered that he was a security consultant who had recently retired from the CIA. The magic letters CIA had a galvanizing impact on a local reporter for the *Washington Post*, Bob Woodward. Bail was set but none of the arrested men could meet it and they were taken to prison.

The official White House line was that Watergate, in the words of Nixon's press secretary, Ron Ziegler, was a 'third rate burglary attempt' and hardly worth serious attention. At the same time, however, presidential meetings were held to discuss how to contain the embryonic scandal. Liddy and others were energetically engaged in shredding files and records that might incriminate the administration.

The accounts of who did what and who said what to whom in the Watergate cover-up are confused and contradictory. But it emerged that John Dean, the legal counsel to President Nixon, became the 'damage control officer' and he quickly involved himself in organizing secret payments to the Watergate burglars to ensure their silence. Dean also assumed responsibility for the contents of Hunt's safe which included the Ellsberg material and other 'dirty tricks' information.

On 23 June, Haldeman had a meeting with Nixon and explained what had been happening with Watergate. In particular, they discussed suggesting that it was a CIA operation and one that the FBI should not pursue beyond the actual burglars. This proposition was put to the Acting Director of the FBI, Patrick Gray, by the Deputy Director of the CIA. In the meantime, it was necessary to use secret campaign contributions to keep the burglars quiet and to find a way of stopping the investigation from going any higher in the hierarchy than Liddy. For some time, it seemed that these strategies had been successful. The FBI and the federal prosecutors were aware of the virtual certainty of Nixon's re-election and it is likely that this 'emboldened the president's men and intimidated their pursuers'.[6] The Acting FBI Director, Gray, actively co-operated with John Dean at the White House and helped ensure that the investigation did not become a 'fishing expedition' for evidence not directly related to the burglary. The mindset of some of those involved is illuminated by one senior official's recollection, 'We were not covering up a burglary; we were safeguarding world peace'.[7]

On 29 August, Nixon was confident enough to claim that no one in his administration was involved in Watergate. He went on to say that, in such matters of overzealous campaigning, 'what really hurts is if you try to cover it up'. John Dean, who was *de facto* in charge of the cover-up, was startled to hear Nixon claim that Dean had carried out a complete investigation of Watergate for him. Dean began to be concerned that he was being set up by Nixon.

Senior officials in the White House were increasingly concerned with finding secret 'hush' money for the Watergate defendants. Some of the defendants were pressing for more explicit commitments of clemency and pardons. But such action could come only from the president and, even then, only after conviction and sentence. The major fly in the White House ointment was McCord, who was unwilling to go along with the cover story that Watergate had been a CIA operation.

In January 1973, the trial of United States v. Liddy et al. opened with Judge John Sirica presiding.[8] Sirica's judicial record was undistinguished and his judgements were frequently overturned by the Court of Appeals. He was well known for the severity of his sentencing and had acquired the nickname of 'Maximum John'. At a pre-trial hearing he made it clear that he wanted to know who had hired the Watergate burglars and why. Hunt and the Miami based burglars, Barker, Gonzales, Martinez and Sturgis all changed their pleas to guilty. On 30 January 1973, Liddy and McCord were found guilty but Judge Sirica was not happy and complained that evidence had been withheld. He delayed sentence in the expectation that the convicted men would be more forthcoming.

In February, 1973 the Senate voted unanimously 77–0 to establish a

Select Committee on Presidential Campaign Activities, under the chairmanship of Sam Ervin of North Carolina. Nixon and his senior staff began to plan a containment strategy to deal with this new Watergate Committee. The central plank of this strategy was to ensure that, by claiming executive privilege, White House staff did not have to appear before the Committee. But this manoeuvre was undermined by the nomination of Acting Director Patrick Gray to be Director of the FBI. At Gray's confirmation hearings, he astonished the Senate Judiciary Committee by telling them that he had given John Dean full access to the Watergate investigation, including allowing him to sit in on FBI interviews. Suddenly, John Dean, President Nixon's counsel, was in the full glare of congressional and media attention. Again invoking the executive privilege strategy, President Nixon announced that he would not let his counsel testify before a congressional committee. Gray's testimony had finished his nomination chances and, in a memorable Watergate phrase, Erlichman advised Dean, 'Let him (Gray) hang there; let him twist slowly, slowly in the wind'.[9]

The three questions to which the White House needed answers were how to keep the burglary team quiet, who to blame for the burglary and how to manage the Ervin Committee. The first required money, parole and possibly pardons. The second looked increasingly like John Mitchell, Director of CRP and some of his staff. The third could be managed by supplying written depositions, rather than testifying on camera. In Fred Emery's words, 'the White House would be preserved by a cover-up of the cover-up'.[10]

While the White House machinations were going on, James McCord, the CRP security consultant and Watergate burglar, delivered a letter to Judge John Sirica. On 23 March, Judge Sirica read from the letter in open court. The letter was to prove fatal to the cover-up in that it claimed political pressure had been exerted on the defendants, that perjury had occurred and that guilty men had not been named. It also denied the claim that the break-in was a CIA operation. Sirica announced he would hear more evidence from McCord and proceeded to sentence the others. The sentences were severe in the extreme. Liddy got twenty years. The Cuban Americans got forty years each and Hunt thirty-five years. In all cases, except Liddy's, the sentences were 'provisional' and would be reviewed in three months and might be adjusted in the light of their co-operation with the Ervin Committee. Within the day, McCord had contacted Sam Dash, the chief counsel to the Ervin Committee to tell him of the involvement of others, including Magruder, the Deputy Director of CRP, Dean and Mitchell.

These revelations caused consternation in the White House and prompted the president's counsel, John Dean, to make urgent and secret plans for his own survival. Dean hired a criminal lawyer who made informal contact with the prosecutor's office to offer information pending a 'plea bargain'. Dean's determination not to become the principal scapegoat for Watergate was such that he was ready to implicate everyone in the White House and CRP. At the same time, Magruder's lawyers were also seeking a plea-bargain arrangement. In effect, Magruder would provide some corroboration for the amazing tale Dean had to tell the prosecutors. Nixon, Haldeman and Erlichman did not know immediately that Dean and Magruder were talking directly to the prosecutors, they were more concerned that Howard Hunt was going to reveal all to a Watergate grand jury. They clung to the idea that Mitchell should take responsibility for everything.

On 15 April, Nixon realized that Dean had betrayed him and that the noose was tightening around his key advisers, Haldeman and Erlichman, in the form of a possible obstruction of justice charge. While Nixon hesitated to sack Dean for fear Dean would directly implicate him in Watergate, Dean was disclosing the original Huston plan and the Watergate burglars' involvement in the burglary of Ellsberg's psychiatrist. Nixon had to act before the criminal justice system turned on him.

Nixon asked for Dean's resignation but Dean said he would go only if Haldeman and Erlichman also resigned. Nixon was in a quandary: if Dean got immunity from the prosecutors, he could bring down the presidency; if Dean did not get immunity, he would have every incentive as a defendant to implicate everyone up to and including Nixon. He decided to oppose immunity in the expectation that the prospect of a presidential pardon would make Dean less likely to turn against his president. Nixon made a press and television statement which offered qualified co-operation with the Ervin Committee and gave a veiled warning to Dean that he opposed giving immunity from prosecution to any senior staff implicated in Watergate.

On 30 April 1973, Nixon broadcast to the nation. He stressed 'we must maintain the integrity of the White House, and the integrity must be real not transparent. There can be no whitewash at the White House.' The resignations of Haldeman and Erlichman, and of the Attorney

General Kleindienst, were announced along with the dismissal of John Dean. Nixon's approval ratings fell from 60 per cent to 45 per cent.

The demand for a special prosecutor, independent of the Justice Department was hard to resist any longer, and Nixon said the appointee would have the full co-operation of the executive branch. Nixon could have appointed a prosecutor of his own choosing long before but it was now too late. By waiting too long, Nixon had lost control of the choice. In replacing Kleindienst with Elliot Richardson as Attorney-General, Nixon ensured that the Democratic majority in the Senate confirmation hearing extracted from Richardson an unprecedented degree of independence for the special prosecutor. But Nixon never imagined that Richardson would choose as special prosecutor Professor Archibald Cox, who had served as Solicitor-General in the Kennedy administration. To make matters even worse for Nixon, almost no boundaries were placed on Cox's investigations and he was not even obliged to inform or consult Attorney-General Richardson.

The first impact of Cox's appointment was to delay the criminal cases, and one consequence was that the floor was left open to Sam Ervin and his Senate Watergate Committee. It was agreed that Dean's testimony would be crucial and he was granted immunity for the statements he gave at the Senate hearings. This forced the prosecution to assemble their own case against Dean before he testified. Live televised hearings began on 17 May 1973,[11] and soon became compelling viewing for millions of Americans. During McCord's testimony, President Nixon put out another statement. He acknowledged some facts he had previously tried to conceal; for example, the Plumbers unit, wiretapping and the Huston plan, but he insisted he would not resign. He also changed his position on executive privilege in that he was prepared to allow present and past staff to appear before the Ervin Committee but privilege would be invoked to prevent access to White House documents and tape recordings.

The star witness before the Ervin Committee was John Dean[12] who testified for five days and, in so doing, directly implicated President Nixon in the Watergate cover-up. The interrogation of Dean allowed the Republican Vice Chair of the Ervin Committee, Howard Baker, to pose the famous question which symbolizes the Watergate scandal and which has been posed in many later scandals, 'what did the President know and when did he know it?'. Presumably, Baker was seeking to demonstrate that Nixon at least did not have prior knowledge of the burglaries at the Watergate. But the answers given by Dean were detailed and damaging. There was no doubting the gravity of the charges he levelled against President Nixon but Ervin and the committee were anxious to have corroboration. On Monday, 16 July 1973, a White House aide, Alexander Butterfield, testified that there was a comprehensive taping system in place in the Oval Office and in other presidential offices which recorded all conversations. It now appeared that Dean's claims and Nixon's denials could be checked against the taped records and, almost immediately, Nixon received requests from both the Ervin Committee and from Special Prosecutor Archibald Cox to hear certain tapes. Nixon refused on the now increasingly familiar ground of privilege. The battle for the tapes had begun.

President Nixon recruited a constitutional adviser, Professor Charles Wright, who argued that presidents had inherent rights to withhold material from courts. Cox swiftly went to Judge Sirica to obtain a subpoena for specific tapes and documents. Nixon refused to comply. Judge Sirica promptly ordered that Nixon show cause why the tapes should not be produced as evidence. In August, Nixon gave another television address which again argued for executive privilege in regard to the tapes. In a televised news conference, the first for more than a year, Nixon expressed confidence that Haldeman and Erlichman would be exonerated.

Judge Sirica ruled against Nixon on the tapes but decided that he should first determine what was or was not covered by executive privilege before a grand jury heard the tapes. Both Nixon and Cox appealed and, in September, the US Court of Appeals produced another variation by proposing that Cox, Wright and Nixon or his representative should listen to the tapes. This was not acceptable to either party.

In the middle of this particular crisis, Nixon had to contend with another scandal in his administration, the allegations of bribery against Vice-President Spiro Agnew. Agnew was reluctant to resign and he briefly sought to mobilize impeachment charges against himself but, on 10 October, he resigned and pleaded no contest to a charge of income tax evasion.[13]

Nixon then decided it was time to put an end to the Watergate scandal and the litigation of the tapes. To protect himself he needed to destroy the Special Prosecutor, Archibald Cox. The Court of Appeal had ordered Nixon to hand over the tapes to Judge Sirica to review on 12 October, and he had only a week to appeal to the Supreme Court. Nixon proposed that, instead of handing over the actual tapes, he would deliver summaries of the tapes verified by an independent third party. The third party he had in mind was Senator John Stennis, the Democrat Chairman of the Armed Services Committee. This proposal was allegedly put to, and accepted by, Senators Ervin and Baker. Cox's response was to say that, while summaries might be adequate for a grand jury, any resulting criminal trial would demand the actual tapes. Nixon's counsel refused to countenance releasing any portion of the tapes and he sought to preclude future access to other tapes and documents of presidential conversations not specified in the original subpoena. Cox was ordered not to make any further attempts to obtain such evidence.

The White House issued a press statement addressing the Stennis Compromise and the order to Cox. Cox immediately issued a counter-statement concluding 'It is my judgement the President is refusing to comply with the court'.[14] It was clear that Cox was not prepared to be coerced into accepting the Stennis proposal. At this point the compromise unravelled. Senators Ervin and Stennis said they had agreed to accept only authenticated whole transcripts and not summaries. At a press conference on Saturday, 20 October, Cox argued that the President was not complying with the court order and that, in any event, only the Attorney-General had the authority to dismiss him. Nixon's counsel immediately asked Attorney-General Elliott Richardson to dismiss Cox. Richardson declined and asked to see Nixon.

The so-called 'Saturday Night Massacre' was one of the most dramatic episodes in America's most dramatic political scandal. At the end of it, the Special Prosecutor Cox had been dismissed, Attorney-General Richardson had resigned along with the Deputy Attorney-General Ruckelshaus. Richardson and Ruckelshaus had refused to dismiss Cox because they believed they had pledged non-interference when confirmed by the Senate. The actual dismissal was carried out by Robert Bork, the Solicitor-General, who also assumed responsibility for returning the functions of the Watergate Special Prosecutor force back to the Department of Justice.

The 'Massacre' caused a public uproar and choruses of indignation and complaint. The sealing of the Special Prosecutor's Office by the FBI suggested to one commentator that 'there was a whiff of the Gestapo in the chill October air'.[15] The stakes had been raised and, whatever the real weather, the political temperature on Capitol Hill was rising. When Congress reconvened on the Tuesday following the 'Massacre', impeachment was in the air. The Speaker of the House, Carl Albert, announced that motions for impeachment had been referred to the House Judiciary committee. This was only the second time in American history that such a referral had been ordered. The Republican leader in the House was Gerald Ford, the new vice-president designate, and Ford agreed to the impeachment referral. Nixon's reluctance to give up the tapes had placed an intolerable strain on erstwhile Republican supporters in the House of Representatives.

Nixon and his advisers belatedly agreed to hand the actual tapes to Judge Sirica as ordered by the Court of Appeals. While the details remained to be decided, the incriminating evidence was to be surrendered to the criminal justice system. To compound matters, Leon Jaworski was appointed as the new Special Prosecutor and he was to prove as independent and troublesome to Nixon as Archibald Cox had been. Having agreed to hand over the nine subpoenaed tapes, the Nixon White House now had the challenging task of explaining to Judge Sirica and Jaworski that two of the tapes did not exist. The missing tapes served to fuel demands for resignation and impeachment. The next White House 'discovery' was that one of the subpoenaed tapes had an eighteen-minute gap on it and it did not appear the erasure could be accidental.

On 1 March 1974, indictments were handed down against some of the most important men in the Nixon administration, Mitchell, Haldeman and Erlichman, charging them with conspiracy to obstruct justice. The demands for new additional tapes continued, both from Jaworski and, in April, from the House Judiciary Committee. In the face of these demands, Nixon persisted with the notion of offering edited tape transcripts. In a television address, Nixon announced that he was making public transcripts of forty-six taped conversations, but the release of these inflamed, rather than appeased, public, political and media opinion. It was not just that the transcripts were incriminating but they revealed a president whose conversations were coarse and undignified.

Nixon was adamant that no one would receive any more tapes and, once again, Jaworski followed in Cox's well-trodden path to ask that another subpoena for tapes be enforced by the court. Sirica again ordered enforcement and, although the White House took the case to the Court of Appeal, they were outmanoeuvred by Jaworski who asked the Supreme Court of the United States to decide the issue as soon as possible. On 31 May 1974 the Supreme Court agreed to consider the issue and a hearing date was set for 8 July for the case of the United States of America v. Richard M. Nixon.

As one track of the Watergate scandal wound its way through the judicial system, another track, the impeachment process started making its way through Congress. The case against Nixon was prepared by John Doar, counsel to the House Judiciary Committee. The Democratic leadership was keen to avoid giving the impeachment process a partizan appearance and searched for consensus. The Judiciary Committee deliberations began in late January and lasted until almost the end of July.

Before the House Committee voted on the articles of impeachment, the Supreme Court decided 8–0 against Nixon and upheld the Jaworski subpoena. Doors were closing on the president. He had exhausted the judicial process and all he could contemplate on the legal front was simply to defy the authority of the Supreme Court. Nixon waited eight hours before confirming that he accepted the court's decision.

When the Judiciary Committee finally finished its work in framing the articles of impeachment, the allegations against President Nixon reached far beyond Watergate, but it was the Watergate-related charges that produced majorities to impeach.[16] Article 1 alleged obstruction of justice and passed 27–11; Article 2, the abuse of power including the use of government agencies against individuals passed 28–10; Article 3, the refusal to comply with Watergate related subpoenas issued by the Judiciary Committee passed 21–17. The two other articles, Article 4 which related to concealing the bombing in Cambodia, and Article 5 which related to illicit personal gains and tax fraud, were both defeated 26–12. On the final day of voting, 30 July, the first of the much-disputed tapes was delivered to Judge Sirica.

On 5 August three more tapes were released and these clearly demonstrated both Nixon's early knowledge of the involvement of his staff in the Watergate burglary and his active role in the cover-up. The tape of 23 June 1972, became known as 'the smoking gun', the incontrovertible proof of Nixon's culpability and complicity in Watergate. The eleven Republicans on the House Judiciary Committee who had opposed impeachment now realized they had been deceived and expressed their support for impeachment proceedings. Nixon had been abandoned by his supporters in Congress and there now seemed little doubt that the impeachment would succeed.

On 9 August, Richard Nixon resigned the Office of President of the United States. A month later, on 8 September, President Gerald Ford granted Nixon a full pardon for 'all offenses against the United States'. The Watergate scandal was, as far as Nixon was concerned, at an end.

Nixon's staff were not so fortunate. The Watergate burglar who blew the whistle, James McCord, served four months' imprisonment, while his accomplices received sentences of between twelve and fifteen months. The heaviest sentences were imposed on the organizers of the burglary. Hunt served almost three years and Liddy four-and-a-half years in prison. Numerous White House and CRP staff were indicted and convicted of Watergate-related offences. At the highest levels of the White House and CRP, John Mitchell, former Attorney-General, served nineteen months while Bob Haldeman and John Erlichman each served eighteen months. Nixon's nemesis, John Dean, was sentenced to one year in prison but served only four months.

In a relatively brief narrative, it is difficult to give a full account of the complexities, ambiguities and contradictions of the Watergate scandal. It seems likely that we will never know the precise role of the CIA and other intelligence agencies, or be able to apportion blame and responsibility entirely accurately.[17] But the intention here is not to unravel competing chronologies and interpretations but to explain Watergate as an example, the leading example, of a political scandal in the United States.

What was it that was scandalous about Watergate? Was it the burglary itself or the cover-up? Or was it the insight the tapes gave to the tone and character of the Nixon administration itself? Unlike some later scandals, it cannot be denied that Watergate attracted immense public attention and overwhelming media coverage. The final act of the drama saw the first-ever resignation of an American president, a man who had won the electoral college votes of forty-nine of the fifty states less than two years earlier.

Electoral dirty tricks were not invented by the Nixon administration. From Nixon's perspective, what made Watergate so painful was the way the liberal media had ignored or played down the excesses of his Democrat predecessors. The West Virginia primary, which helped secure Kennedy's nomination, and the counting of votes in certain districts of Illinois in the general election of 1960 have attracted a good deal of subsequent attention. Nixon's predecessor, Johnson, was involved in a Senate race in 1948 which probably still holds the prize as the most corrupt election in American history. In such circumstances, it is understandable that Nixon found it difficult to understand why Watergate was regarded as a serious matter. If the offence itself was trivial and unoriginal, then covering it up could scarcely be a matter for resignation or impeachment.

Watergate was a product of a particular political climate and context. The social and political upheavals caused by the civil rights campaigns and the Vietnam War had driven Johnson from the White House, and Nixon, the veteran anti-communist, was determined to crack down on subversives and dissenters. Anyone who opposed the Vietnam War was seen as unpatriotic and should be dealt with accordingly. The emergence of McGovern as a front runner for the Democrat nomination, possibly as a stalking horse for Ted Kennedy, signified the gulf between the parties. Nixon saw McGovern as an ultra-liberal, a 'peacenik', who would surrender to the onward march of international communism. His election would be a tragedy for the nation and it was Nixon's duty to use all means to ensure it did not happen. Distrusting existing agencies and especially the autonomy of the FBI under J. Edgar Hoover, Nixon wanted his own political intelligence unit which would do his bidding. Those who staffed and directed this unit were the president's men, and 'loyalty to the President was equated with loyalty to the nation and the re-election of the President became synonymous with the public good'.[18]

Thus the Watergate burglary was not an isolated, deviant event carried out by overzealous, renegade staff but rather a part of a pattern of surveillance and 'dirty tricks'. If Nixon did not invent 'dirty tricks', he did institutionalize them in the White House. This institutionalization was part of a larger effort to increase the power of the White House *vis-à-vis* Congress and government departments. Nixon made a serious effort to run the federal government from the White House, and his top aides became ever more powerful as they became more like political executives and less like mere advisers and facilitators. In his own mind, Nixon was crystal clear about this strategy and noted, 'I had thrown down a gauntlet to Congress, the bureaucracy, the media and the Washington establishment and challenged them to engage in epic battle'.[19]

Having struggled to break the bonds of the political system and, in so doing condoned illegal acts, Nixon was short of friends and supporters when Watergate began to unravel. Having failed to take over the system, Nixon was broken by the system. As the scandal unfolded, Nixon tried and failed to control the criminal investigation. Despite interference from the Attorney-General and his deputy, the federal prosecutors continued to develop cases against members of the White House staff.

The so called 'liberal media' had a field day but it should be remembered that, for long periods, the Watergate scandal was important only to a few newspapers and even they often relegated it to the inside pages. If President Nixon was unable to control effectively all the elements of the executive branch, it is hardly surprising that Congress, the judiciary and a free press remained beyond his reach. Nixon was fond of describing himself as a fighter but one problem with fighting is that opponents usually hit back. Newspaper and television headlines, congressional inquiries, federal prosecutors, judicial hearings and court orders all played their parts in developing the Watergate scandal from its beginning as a 'third rate burglary'.

Watergate is an important political scandal, not merely because of its dramatic consequences, but for the light it sheds on how such scandals develop and are sustained. It emphasizes that American political scandals do not usually have a single focus, but rather they are multi-centred. Inquiries, allegations and disclosures emanate from multiple sources in a fragmented and porous political system. The spotlight of publicity moves from media reports to FBI investigators, to court hearings to special prosecutors to congressional committees and back again. This has the effect of multiplying the pressures on those caught up in the scandal, and they are forced to fight on several fronts at once. Defensive tactics which are effective in one arena, such as refusing to testify to a congressional committee, are unlikely to be appropriate in a courtroom setting. Responding to news stories, the demands of federal investigators and complying with court and congressional subpoenas and proceedings takes an increasing amount of time for an increasing number of senior people. Accounts have to be collated and co-ordinated, and care has to be taken that, when escaping from one predicament, the administration is not placed in a worse situation. In particular, jumping from the pan of adverse publicity into the fire of litigation is usually unwise.

If most scandals are characterized by a cover-up, what was earlier termed a procedural scandal, Watergate demonstrates how difficult they are to devise and to manage. There are too many loose ends to tie up and too many loose cannons to control. The more people who are involved in the substantive scandal, the more likely it is that the cover-up will be impossible to sustain. The 'cancer' of Watergate spread upwards in the White House because the lower level operatives did not have the resources, contacts or authority to meet the 'hush money' and legal fees required by the burglars. The more people who knew about the payments, the more likely it was that the story would 'leak' out or be extracted by the threat of prosecution.

Covering up a scandal is not only difficult but it requires time and preparation. In Watergate it sometimes seemed as if participants were making it up as they went along. The lack of preparation was strikingly obvious both in the way the Watergate burglaries were carried out and in the way the White House tried to employ a cover story which one of the burglars publicly rejected. As a scandal breaks there is a real difficulty for those involved in establishing the facts, in developing a chronology and in finding non-incriminating explanations which are consistent with the facts and chronology as understood at the time. New facts emerge, old 'facts' prove to be wrong, there are conflicting accounts and the chronology becomes confused.

It is sometimes the case that those in charge of cover ups simply make errors of judgement. They misread the public mood, for example, the final disclosure of tapes did not encourage the American public to commend President Nixon for his frankness but rather their tone and content revealed that the emperor had no clothes. The illusions of the presidency, the power of an electoral mandate, were stripped away and Nixon was demeaned in the process. In the Watergate scandal, Nixon seems to have succumbed to the belief that, as president, he was immune to prosecution, and as commander-in-chief, his staff would happily lay down their careers and their liberty to protect him. But the persistence of the prosecutors and the threat of imprisonment concentrated the minds and weakened the resolve of almost all the president's men.

At first prosecutors met a wall of denial but, once the wall was breached, the entire edifice was compromised. When the floods of Watergate poured through, the survivors scrambled for the life-rafts available to those willing to implicate others in the 'dirty tricks' and the cover-up. As soon as John Dean realized that the horrors of Watergate were to be laid at his door, he sought immunity or at least a reduction and dilution of the potential charges in exchange for full co-operation. The existence of the tapes and their eventual production provided in-dependent evidence that Dean's testimony was true and Nixon's denials were lies. The game was up and Nixon resigned because he had lost almost all Republican support in Congress, and impeachment was inevit-able. Nixon had always had his share of enemies but, in the last days of Watergate, he had precious few friends.

Watergate, like many other political scandals, had an inauspicious beginning. It began slowly and attracted little public, media and political attention. Its implications, its scale and its gravity were not understood by either the investigators or the investigated. Once arrested, the burglars, together with Hunt and Liddy, were obviously under pressure but they had expectations that they and their families would be looked after. They hoped the prosecutions would be dropped and, failing that, representations to the judge would produce light sentences. If the worst came to the worst, there was always the prospect of a presidential pardon. The presence and background of James McCord clearly aroused the interest of Judge Sirica and of the *Washington Post* team, Woodward and Bernstein. But after Nixon's crushing victory in the presidential election of 1972, the 'third rate burglary' seemed trivial and inconsequential, and explicable in terms of a lack of judgement by overzealous campaign staff. But this was not an isolated burglary, there was the earlier burglary of the Watergate building, the burglary of Ellsberg's psychiatrist and other matters. If one burglary could be dismissed as an isolated lapse, two, three or more looked like rather more than carelessness or campaigning zeal. The need to prevent prosecutors, judges and press from making these connections is what motivated the cover-up and implicated the White House.

What was potentially scandalous was not a single burglary but an orchestrated campaign of political espionage. The need to conceal this produced the cover-up and the gradual breaking-down of the cover-up is what sustained the scandal as it reached higher and higher in the Nixon administration. As a public drama, Watergate offered live congressional hearings, sensational press headlines and the spectacle of the Justice Department imploding during the 'Saturday Night Massacre'. It was clear that, to survive, the president would have to purge his entire administration including some of 'the finest public servants' [20] he had ever known but the tapes proved that the damage-limitation exercise had its limits. The tapes of erstwhile secret presidential conversations became public property, transcripts became best-selling books and the phrase 'expletive deleted' entered the language. Ninety per cent of the American public watched at least part of the Ervin Committee hearings and, once a scandal becomes public property, it has to run its course, the genie cannot be put back in the bottle.

The culmination of the Watergate scandal, the resignation of Richard Nixon, was seen by many conservatives as a *coup d'état* engineered by the liberal media and Nixon's Democrat opponents in Congress and the judiciary. In this view the real scandal of Watergate was the failure to expose this conspiracy against President Nixon. They seize upon Hougan's argument that the Watergate burglary was a CIA plot against the administration. They insist that other presidents committed worse crimes and claim the scandalmongers succeeded in securing by conspiracy what they had singularly failed to secure at the ballot box, the defeat of Nixon. The English conservative, Paul Johnson, asserted that Watergate was 'the first media putsch in history, as ruthless and anti-democratic as any military coup by bemedaled generals with their sashes and sabres'.[21] From this perspective, Watergate did not involve any scandalous crimes or provoke a constitutional crisis but rather was artificially created and hyped by the many enemies of President Nixon. The conservative critics are correct to argue that Nixon's liberal opponents were happy to use the Watergate burglaries as a club to beat on Nixon but what they find more difficult to explain is the extended cover-up. Nixon was not hounded from office because of electoral 'dirty tricks' but because of his attempts to conceal his responsibility and, in so doing, to deceive Congress, the courts and the public.

If extreme conservatives see Nixon as the victim of the Watergate scandal, those on the left tend to see him as the scapegoat who distracted public attention from more fundamental abuses of political power. The Watergate revelations were, in Chomsky's words, 'analogous to the discovery that the directors of Murder Inc. were also cheating on their income tax'.[22] While the right demonizes the press for persecuting Nixon, the radical left indicts the press as co-conspirators for their failure to address broader issues of greater significance. From this perspective, Watergate was but a symptom of a wider malaise in the American political system which could not be cured simply by purging a handful of individuals. The malaise was the growth and abuse of executive power which both preceded Watergate and extended far beyond it. A media focus on Nixon and his immediate cronies did nothing to explain Watergate in its appropriate political context. This omission made explicit by the failure of the one article of impeachment, Article 4, which sought to impeach Nixon on the grounds that he prosecuted a secret war in a neutral country without congressional authorization. To left-wing critics, President Nixon was forced from office over trivial misdemeanours while serious felonies were ignored.

The mainstream reaction to Watergate differed markedly from more radical interpretations. It focused more on alleged law-breaking than with political conspiracies. It tended to the view that Nixon's crimes were serious and different, not trivial and familiar as the extreme right would have it, but also that they were aberrations, the product of political paranoia and not, as the left would have it, the result of major structural faults in the American political system. Within the mainstream, there were differences of view but the major newspapers and most members of Congress saw Watergate as a gross abuse of presidential power. Where there were differences, they centred less on the scandalous events themselves and more on the lessons or conclusions to be drawn from them.

Moderate Republicans argued that, shocking as the misdeeds were, they were uncovered and those culpable brought to justice. The FBI, the Justice Department attorneys, the special prosecutors, the grand jury, Judge Sirica, the Supreme Court, Senator Sam Ervin and his committee and a free press all played their parts in uncovering the truth of Watergate and identifying those responsible for it. In other words, the system worked. President Nixon's misdeeds were exposed and he was held accountable to the constitution and the laws of the land. This reaffirmation of the United States as governed by law rather than by people encouraged the belief that there were no structural, constitutional, or procedural lessons to be learned from the Watergate scandal. The system had been threatened but had demonstrated the capacity to meet and to overcome the threat.

Democrats and editorial writers were more concerned with how close the Nixon White House came to getting away with it. If McCord had not been chosen as a burglar, if reporters less driven than Woodward and Bernstein had been involved, if a judge less curious and idiosyncratic than Sirica had been assigned to the case and if a more pliable special prosecutor and attorney-general had been appointed, Watergate might well have become a footnote in a history of electoral 'dirty tricks'. Although the system worked in this case, it did so by accident and good fortune. The lesson that most liberals drew from the scandal was the importance of enacting reform measures designed to preclude or at least inhibit recurrence. One 'long national nightmare' [23] was enough, and the horrors exposed during Watergate encouraged good citizens to find ways of curbing and containing the potentially unconstitutional ambitions of Nixon's successors in the White House. From this perspective, the Watergate scandal served to justify and legitimate a whole raft of reform measures which would otherwise have been thought unnecessary and almost impossible to see enacted.

Mainstream opinion was therefore divided as to whether a Watergate-type scandal could occur again but the fact that it had occurred once gave the impetus and political advantage to the reformers. Republicans who wanted to believe Watergate was a one-off were also drawn to the idea of a pattern of wrongdoing by Nixon's Democrat predecessors and this weakened their opposition to reform. After Watergate, the presidency was briefly more imperilled than imperial. Congress was resurgent and the legislative agenda included campaign finance reform, the independent counsel law and the War Powers Act. The issue of presidential accountability came to prominence, and presidential candidate, Jimmy Carter, 'used Watergate as a platform for placing ethical behavior at the center of his political identity, thereby helping to establish the moral accountability of public officials as a central issue on the national political agenda'.[24]

To the general public, the Watergate scandal was a drama and a spectacle. The drama was in turn tragic and comic, and televized hearings allowed the entire nation to be a part of the audience. Unlike some later scandals, Watergate was a relatively simple story to tell and the witnesses who told it became public personalities. It was relatively easy to distinguish the good guys from the bad, the heroes from the villains. Such judgements were derived from the outcome. President Nixon was the bad guy and those who brought him down were righteous soldiers defending the republic and the constitution. The popular images of Watergate cast key figures in heroic roles at the expense of a more balanced evaluation. In this sense, the Watergate scandal was another example of 'American culture's long-standing inclination to translate political complexities into moral simplicities'.[25]

The heroes of Watergate, Senator Sam Ervin, Judge John Sirica, Attorney-General Elliott Richardson and Special Prosecutor Archibald Cox are an interestingly diverse group in terms of their attitudes, temperaments and social origins. Ervin, the epitome of the courtly southern gentleman, won almost universal approval for the conduct of the Senate hearings. His defence of and respect for constitutional propriety were in stark contrast to the highly pragmatic and unprincipled evidence of many witnesses. Liberals elevated Ervin almost to iconic status and, for Watergate purposes, conveniently forgot his racist attitudes and long-standing opposition to civil rights legislation. It is often forgotten that Ervin's days of public glory would have been denied to him if another Watergate hero, Archibald Cox, had had his way. Cox sought unsuccessfully to exclude the television cameras from the Senate hearings for fear of their possible prejudicial effect on later criminal trials.

Judge John Sirica was an equally unlikely liberal hero: a lifelong Republican known for his conservative views and draconian sentencing policies. His judicial record was distinguished mainly by the number of successful appeals from his court. His respect for his judicial colleagues in the Court of Appeal was limited. In Sirica's view, Appeal Court reversals did not mean he was wrong, 'it just means they've got the last word on you'.[26] Sirica's choice of tactics in dealing with the Watergate burglars is open to question. To announce maximum sentences of several decades' duration as a way of ensuring co-operation with a congressional committee is the sort of coercion which normally meets with liberal disapproval. But Sirica's pressure worked and McCord's letter to him opened up the Watergate inquiries. In political scandals, as in competitive sports, it seems the result is everything, or at least getting the bad guys compensates for whatever reservations there may be about the means employed. Sirica's role in the history of Watergate is assured. His persistence and determination to get to the bottom of the matter may well have exceeded his brief but his stubborn refusal to buckle in the face of White House pressure ensures that any judicial lapses were easily condoned.

The story of the Watergate scandal is thus partly a story of individuals with striking characteristics: Nixon and his obsession with enemies; Ervin playing the good guy in the white suit; Sirica personifying the independence of the judiciary. These individuals helped create and define the scandal, and it is easy to imagine how different the story might have been if other individuals had played these parts. But a political scandal involves more than the sum of the idiosyncrasies of the key players. It involves ideological conflict, institutional confrontations and partisan rivalries. It starts in one institutional location and is picked up by the press and other institutions. The scandal develops momentum, it multiplies and diversifies. In one sense, institutions compete for the heart of the scandal. Newspapers use banner headlines, television exploits a captive mass audience, courts hand out subpoenas and sentences, Congress holds hearings in both houses, prosecutors investigate and interrogate and those implicated prepare for the siege or seek a way out.

In Watergate, as in other scandals, no one institution or individual controls the unfolding of the scandal. Scandals have multiple facets and multiple narratives. There is no one story but several unco-ordinated lines of inquiry pursued in parallel. What distinguishes Watergate is the 'smoking gun' which eliminated the 'plausible denial' and the partial admission or, as Erlichman termed it, the 'modified, limited hang-out'.[27] Each player pursues its own institutional logic and priorities. Each feeds on the revelations unearthed by others that, collectively, undermine the inadequacies and half-truths of official denials.

But it is important not to interpret political scandals with hindsight. The Watergate break-in could have been a 'third rate burglary' and none of the key players had a grasp of the full plot, let alone a preview of the scandal's denouement. The power and publicity generated by political scandals are now well understood by politicians, the press and the public but Watergate was the first of its kind and not all understood the dangers and opportunities it presented. The Senate agreed by unanimous vote to set up its Select Committee on Presidential Campaign Activities, (the Ervin Committee), but Senators were not exactly pushing hard to become embroiled in a confrontation with the President of the United States. This meant that the committee was small (seven members) and each member was able to attract a good deal of media attention. The Ervin Committee's role was judged heroic in the court of public opinion and this triumph has had profound implications for the scale and structure of congressional inquiries into subsequent political scandals. The Iran–Contra Committee had almost four times as many members as the Senate Watergate Committee.

This chapter has explored the causes, the anatomy and some of the more striking consequences of Watergate. But does the enduring importance of Watergate lie in the events themselves, momentous as they were, in the precedents and legal framework it established, the images it employed, or in the vocabulary it created? In short, is it possible to discuss political scandals in the United States without harking back to Watergate? Do modern scandals pose the same questions and demand similar investigatory mechanisms? Put differently, having institutionalized scandal-hunting, is its use inescapable? In particular, is the investigation of scandal always to be confined to criminal wrongdoing by high officials? President Nixon's conflicts with Congress over policy in South-east Asia formed an important part of the political context of Watergate but Congress chose to focus on common crimes rather than on the issue of constitutional usurpation. Significantly, Article Four of the impeachment document was rejected 26–12 by the House Judiciary Committee. As will be seen in Chapter 3 on Iran–Contra, this congressional precedent of focusing on illegality was to be followed in later scandals. The attempt to expand presidential prerogatives went largely unaddressed. While all can agree a crime is a crime, particularly if you have the self-incriminating taped evidence of the alleged culprit, the limits and role of the presidency were too divisive and too partisan to yield a consensus. Like Supreme Court decisions, Ervin's Committee appreciated that unanimity has more clout than reports that reveal partizan or ideological divisions. In Watergate, a consensus developed around the lowest common denominator of public and political opinion, a crook in the White House should be removed.

Contemporary scandals evoke memories of and comparisons with Watergate. To some observers, Watergate has assumed the role of 'pre-emptive metaphor, a past, traumatic experience so compelling it forces itself as the frame for understanding new experiences, even as it ensures a misunderstanding of the new experiences'.[28] Viewing subsequent scandals through Watergate tinted spectacles may, in part, be unavoidable if the participants in those scandals understood their own roles within the framework established by Watergate. But it would be inaccurate to claim that all presidential scandals are variations on the Watergate theme. There are important differences as well as familiar echoes but the political context, the mass media and, to an extent, the political institutions have changed.

Political scandals offer a learning experience to politicians, but avoiding the mistakes of the past is no guarantee of immunity from scandal allegations in the future. If generals are always well prepared to win the war before the one they are actually fighting, politicians have to adapt to the demands of the present. The decline in public trust in politicians which started before Watergate, but was accelerated by it, means that the threshold of scandal has been lowered. Public opinion is more likely to accept that senior politicians and even the president himself may be lying. This increased scepticism of both the media and the public is not the least important legacy of Watergate. It may have been 'under-motivated and overbungled'[29] but Watergate ensured that ambitious legislators and reporters would not be lacking in motivation when a president next found himself immersed in political scandal.

Notes

1. Quoted in Stanley I. Kutler, *The Wars of Watergate: The Last Crisis of Richard Nixon* (New York: Knopf, 1990), p. 559.
2. Tom Charles Huston was a young and relatively junior member of the White House

staff. For details of the Huston Plan and a comparison with Oliver North's role in the Iran–Contra scandal, see L. K. Johnson, 'Mr Huston and Colonel North', *Corruption and Reform*, vol. 3, No. 2, 1988/89, pp. 207–34.

3. Quoted in Fred Emery, *Watergate: the Corruption and Fall of Richard Nixon* (London: Jonathan Cape, 1994), p. 25.

4. In 1967, Secretary of Defense Robert S. McNamara commissioned a major study of how and why the United States had become so deeply involved in Vietnam. The result was a 47-volume report by 36 authors entitled *History of US Decision-Making Process on Vietnam Policy*, which was completed at the end of 1968. Extracts were published in book form: see *The Pentagon Papers (as published by the New York Times)* (New York: Bantam, 1971).

5. There are conflicting accounts of who actually authorized the burglary; Erlichman admits only to authorizing a covert operation to examine Ellsberg's medical records. H. R. Haldeman believes Nixon himself authorized the break-in. See H. R. Haldeman, *The Ends of Power* (London: Book Club Associates, 1978), pp. 113–15.

6. Emery, p. 196.

7. Jeb Stuart Magruder, *An American Life* (New York: Atheneum, 1974), p. 272.

8. Sirica's own account of the trial and the Watergate scandal is set out in John J. Sirica, *To Set the Record Straight* (New York: Norton, 1979).

9. Quoted in Emery, p. 247.

10. Emery, p. 250.

11. U.S. Senate Select Committee on Presidential Campaign Activities, Hearings, *The Final Report*, 93rd Congress, 2nd Session, Washington D.C., 1973–74.

12. For Dean's account of the White House approach to the Watergate scandal, see John Dean, *Blind Ambition: The White House Years* (New York: Simon and Schuster, 1976).

13. Agnew later came to believe that Nixon's lack of support for him was prompted by a desire to appease Attorney General Richardson before Nixon moved against Special Prosecutor, Archibald Cox. See Kutler, pp. 394–7.

14. Quoted in Emery, p. 394.

15. Emery, p. 401. Leon Jaworski, Cox's successor as Special Prosecutor, made a similar Gestapo comparison; see Kutler, p. 406.

16. For an interesting discussion of how the House Judiciary Committee approached the Watergate scandal and the impeachment issue, see L. H. LaRue, *Political Discourse: a case study of the Watergate Affair* (Athens and London: University of Georgia Press, 1988).

17. Some accounts place the CIA at the centre of the Watergate scandal: see Jim Hougan, *Secret Agenda: Watergate, Deep Throat and the CIA* (New York: Random House, 1984).

18. A. S. Markovits and M. Silverstein, *The Politics of Scandal: Power and Process in Liberal Democracies* (New York: Holmes and Meier, 1988), p. 16.

19. Quoted in Kutler, p. xiv. For analysis of Nixon's ambitions for an expanded role for the White House, see Richard Nathan, *The Administrative Presidency*, rev. edn (New York: Wiley, 1983).

20. Nixon's description of Haldeman and Erlichman in a television address on 30 April 1974. See Emery, pp. 345–50.

21. Quoted in M. Schudson, *Watergate in American Memory* (New York: Basic Books, 1992), p. 27.

22. Quoted in Schudson, p. 28.

23. A phrase used by President Ford in his inaugural speech.
24. Schudson, p. 87.
25. Schudson, p. 183.
26. Quoted in Emery, p. 237.
27. Quoted in William H. Chafe and Harvard Sitkoff (eds), *A History of our Times* (New York: Oxford University Press, 1991), p. 434.
28. Schudson, p. 167.
29. Garry Wills, quoted in Schudson, p. 25.

CHAPTER 3

The Iran–Contra Scandal

For American foreign policy, 1979 was a bad year. The coming-to-power of a fundamentalist regime in Iran and the success of the Sandinista revolution in Nicaragua meant the loss of friendly allies and the probable destabilization of the Middle East and Central America. The Reagan administration was alarmed at the prospect of growing Cuban and Soviet influence in Nicaragua and anxious about the possible flow of arms to left-wing rebels in neighbouring El Salvador. In 1981, the administration authorized CIA support and training for the *Contras*, Nicaraguan exiles engaged in a guerrilla war against the Nicaraguan army. In the same year, fifty-two American hostages were released from Iran after more than a year in captivity.

The Reagan administration announced that international terrorism, rather than human rights, would become a foreign policy priority. But, in 1983, 241 American servicemen were killed in a terrorist bombing in Beirut and, a year later in the same city, terrorists started kidnapping Americans and Europeans and demanding the release of their comrades held in other countries, notably Kuwait. The official policy of the United States was that no negotiations should be entered into in case it encouraged further hostage-taking, but the kidnapping and torture of William Buckley, CIA station chief in Beirut, caused particular concern and distress in Washington. The Reagan administration, prompted by Israel, determined it was time to build bridges toward the government in Iran. The escalation of hostage-taking, the state of the Iran–Iraq war and concerns about Soviet influence in the region seem to have been the important catalysts. Working through Israeli and Iranian intermediaries, it was agreed to sell arms to Iran.

Robert McFarlane, the national security adviser,[1] proposed the initiative to Bill Casey, Director of the CIA, who supported it against the opposition of Secretary of State, George Shultz, and Secretary of Defense, Caspar Weinberger. McFarlane and Casey became the chief advocates of weapons sales to Iran. Under President Reagan, the National Security Council staff had assumed roles beyond that of research, advice or co-ordination. At times, it became an operational agency with prime responsibility for what became known as the Iran—Contra operations. McFarlane readily took on operational tasks and delegated some to his deputy director of political-military affairs, Lt-Col. Oliver North. Although McFarlane resigned as national security adviser in December 1985, he stayed in contact with his successor and former deputy, Vice-Admiral John Poindexter, and with North. In due course, Poindexter took over responsibility for supervising North's involvement in arms sales to Iran and in finding funds to support the Contras in Nicaragua.

The sale of arms was organized by a variety of means and through a number of different organizations and intermediaries. To conceal American involvement, arms were initially shipped to Iran by Israel using its own stocks of American-made weapons on the understanding that the Americans would replenish those Israeli stocks. The principal go-between with the Israelis and Iranians was an Iranian citizen, Manuchar Ghorbanifar. Ghorbanifar had previously worked as an agent of SAVAK, the Shah of Iran's secret police, and it might be thought that such an employment record made him an unlikely candidate to mediate with representatives of the new fundamentalist regime in Iran.

The arms sales developed into direct sales to Iran albeit by using a multiplicity of 'cut-outs' intended to disguise the true origin of the weapons. These included the involvement of the CIA and a retired Major-General, Richard Secord, as well as Albert Hakim, an Iranian businessman, who had taken American citizenship in 1984. The CIA were suspicious that Ghorbanifar was an Israeli agent and sceptical of his veracity.[2] National security adviser, Robert McFarlane, travelled to London in December 1985 to meet Ghorbanifar and was reportedly 'revolted' by him. Ghorbanifar was asked to come to Washington and, in January 1986, he underwent a polygraph (lie detector) test. It seems that Ghorbanifar failed on thirteen of the fifteen questions and, in fact, the only questions he appeared to answer truthfully were his name and nationality! Despite this unsatisfactory test result and the desire of senior CIA officers to dispense with Ghorbanifar's services, the CIA Director, Bill Casey, persisted in using him. In Casey's judgement, the Americans had few contacts in Iran who were as well connected as Ghorbanifar and thus the United States government continued to depend on the integrity and discretion of an Iranian former secret policeman to implement a major covert foreign policy initiative. The American dilemma was expressed in a message from McFarlane to Oliver North, 'Gorba is a self-serving mischief maker. The trouble is that as far as we know, so is the entire lot of those we are dealing with'.[3]

The arms sales followed a complicated and evolving pattern. The Department of Defense would sell arms to the CIA; the CIA would re-sell those arms to an armaments company controlled by General Secord; Secord would sell them on to Ghorbanifar and, finally, Ghorbanifar would sell them to Iran. The Israeli role changed from that of supplier to acting as a base for delivery of the weapons and as a possible 'cover' if the arrangements went wrong. The payments followed the reverse route; Iran paid Ghorbanifar, Ghorbanifar paid Secord, Secord paid the CIA and the CIA paid the Department of Defense. The opportunities for corruption, misunderstandings, mistakes and double dealing in such complex transactions are obvious.

But obscuring the paper trail did not meet the immediate need to bring influence to bear on the Iranians and, in May 1986, possibly the most bizarre mission in diplomatic history took place. McFarlane, North and an Israeli official travelled to Tehran using Irish passports. They carried with them gifts, a bible signed by President Reagan and a chocolate cake made by a kosher baker in Tel Aviv. When they arrived, there was no one there to meet them and when, subsequently, negotiations did take place, it was apparent that Ghorbanifar had been saying different things to each side. The negotiations failed and the group decided to leave, presumably without the cake.

At this point it was decided to abandon Ghorbanifar and to use what became known at the 'second channel', believed to be a nephew of Rafsanjani, the Iranian Speaker. Ghorbanifar repeatedly complained about his financial losses and North was warned by the Israelis that Ghorbanifar's money problems and his resentment at being left out of future sales jeopardized the operational security of the Iran arms sales. On 2 November 1986, one hostage, David Jacobsen, was released in response to the delivery of 500 TOW missiles. But public exposure of the arms sales the next day brought the arms-for-hostages operation to a halt.

The plan to sell arms was thought to have a number of benefits. Reagan seems to have believed it would create a new beginning in US–Iran relations. In consequence, the sales would also act as an indirect form of ransom, and the Ayatollah Khomeini would order his followers in Lebanon to release the hostages. Given that the US was also supplying critical military intelligence to Iraq, the Iranian need for American arms supplies could be substantial and long-term. Shipments of missiles began in August 1985 and one hostage was soon released. Reagan had asked that it be Buckley but he had already been tortured to death. The third benefit was that the sales were very profitable because the Iranians were asked to pay two or three times the normal price for the weapons. These arms sales profits were subsequently to be used for the Contra branch of the Iran–Contra scandal.

The Reagan administration's policy of supporting the Contra rebels had soon run into difficulty with Congress. The Contra forces, trained and supplied by the United States, had grown rapidly in size and, by 1982, the prospect of large scale conflict was imminent. While the administration saw Nicaragua as a testing ground for the Reagan doctrine of rolling back Soviet influence in the third world, the media and the Democrats in Congress began to be concerned about the dangers of involving American forces in a guerrilla war, and the spectre of Vietnam loomed in the background. The Contras themselves proved to be a mixed bunch including mercenary units of Cubans and Hondurans and were alleged to have been involved in a number of atrocities. Many members of Congress thought it time to subject this administration's involvement in a secret war to some legislative supervision. This desire formed the impetus for a series of measures, the Boland Amendments,[4] which were later to become key criteria for assessing the behaviour of the administration when the Iran–Contra scandal burst into the newspaper headlines in 1986.

The first Boland Amendment in 1982 was an attempt to involve Congress in Central American policy-making without being seen to undermine President Reagan, betray the Contras or give succour to the Sandinista government in Nicaragua. It accepted at face value the administration's claim that its aims were restricted to encouraging reform in Nicaragua and stopping the supply of arms to El Salvador,[5] and it merely forbade military aid 'for the purpose of overthrowing the government of Nicaragua or provoking a military exchange between Nicaragua and Honduras'.[6] In other words, it attempted to limit the scope of Contra activity rather than deny them arms. It was sufficiently vague and imprecise as to be acceptable to the White House and the Republican-controlled Senate, and it passed the House of Representatives by a vote of 411–0. The Amendment implicitly recognized the Contras and supported certain limited objectives and, in so doing, it established a precedent and a context for subsequent events.

The second Boland Amendment was passed in 1983 and attempted to regulate and make public the amount of money flowing to the Contras. Instead of President Reagan using the CIA contingency fund, Congress insisted on approving a fixed amount in aid. But this Amendment had not long been in place when it was revealed that the CIA was implicated in the mining of Nicaraguan harbours which had resulted in damage to Soviet shipping. Republicans in the Senate felt betrayed by their own side, and Senator Barry Goldwater wrote a memorably pointed letter to the CIA Director recording his dissatisfaction.[7] The growing anxiety about the character and escalation of the war in Nicaragua encouraged the passage of the third, and much more restrictive, Boland Amendment in October 1984. The force of this Amendment was to preclude military aid to the Contras from 'funds available to the Central Intelligence Agency, the Department of Defense or any other agency or entity of the United States involved in intelligence activities'.[8] It was this Amendment the meaning of which would be exhaustively discussed in the Iran–Contra investigations and hearings. North and others would claim that it did not apply to the National Security Council. The third Boland Amendment had given Congress the initiative as the mid-term elections approached, and it prompted concerted efforts by the Reagan administration to sway public opinion and to find other legislative devices for sustaining the flow of aid to the Contras. These were to prove unsuccessful until the Nicaraguan leader, Ortega, visited Moscow in the following year and a fourth Boland Amendment was enacted authorizing $27 million in non-military aid to the Contras. As Foley notes, 'the tide of opinion within Congress had changed. That tide had turned into a flood by the end of 1985',[9] and a fifth and final Boland Amendment was approved which authorized some military aid.

In June 1986, Congress approved $70 million in military aid to the Contras. The Reagan administration's pleasure in overcoming two years of congressional obstruction was somewhat dimmed by the Sandinistas' success in October 1986 in shooting down a military supply plane with an American crew. The surviving crew member, Eugene Hasenfus, confessed to working for the CIA. Bad as this news was, it paled into insignificance when, on 3 November 1986, a Lebanese journal reported the McFarlane/North mission to Tehran. The following day, the Speaker of the Iranian Parliament confirmed the accuracy of the report.

The Iran—Contra scandal was soon in full flow and it quickly engulfed the Reagan administration. The timing could not have been worse because Democrat gains in the November 1986 elections meant that Reagan had now lost the support of the Senate. The Democrats in Congress were ideally placed to gain full benefit from the revelations and repercussions of this Republican scandal.

The considered response of the White House to the Iran—Contra scandal was in marked contrast to the Nixon White House's response to Watergate. This was no 'third rate burglary' and there could be no denying the importance of the issues, and no shirking of White House responsibility. After initial denials and confusion, a press conference was called at which Attorney-General Meese's briefing had to compensate for President Reagan's inadequate and inaccurate grasp of the facts. Meese had gathered the essential facts in a fairly brief period but not before Oliver North and others had destroyed much of the incriminating evidence. Within weeks, the Criminal Division of the Justice Department and the FBI had launched criminal investigations. President Reagan's national security adviser, John Poindexter, resigned and Oliver North was dismissed. Within a month, a presidential commission of inquiry was announced and Attorney-General Meese requested the appointment of an independent counsel to investigate Iran—Contra. This office had been created in the wake of Watergate to avoid a repetition of the 'Saturday Night Massacre' and the dismissal of Special Prosecutor, Archibald Cox.[10] The engines of scandal had been promptly started, put into gear and would have to run their course. In this scandal, the independent counsel did not submit his final report until January 1994 when not only had Reagan left office, but so had his successor, George Bush. No doubt Nixon would have appreciated a similar dilatoriness on the parts of Cox and Jaworski.

Not content with a presidential commission and an independent counsel, the Senate Intelligence Committee called Poindexter and North to appear before it, and both refused to answer questions by invoking the Fifth Amendment protection against self-incrimination. While a succession of Watergate participants testified before the Ervin Committee and, in so doing, implicated others in criminal wrongdoing, North's legal advisers made it crystal clear that North would give testimony to Congress only if he received immunity from prosecution. Independent Counsel, Lawrence Walsh, warned against granting immunity on the grounds that it would jeopardize subsequent prosecutions and make it difficult to establish individual culpability. But Congress was not to be denied its own starring role in what promised to be a bigger and more serious scandal than Watergate. It was determined to receive a first-hand account of North's amazing tale on prime-time television. Iran–Contra was just too important to leave to the protracted and convoluted work-ings of the legal process. President Reagan and his administration were to be called to account by the legislature and nothing would deflect Congress from its constitutional duty.

Given the celebrity status accorded Senator Ervin and his colleagues during Watergate, members of the House of Representatives were equally determined to have their days in the sun, or at least under the television lights. The consequence was that the congressional committee established to investigate the Iran–Contra scandal was a joint committee of both houses and inevitably rather large. It was, in effect, two com-mittees, one from the House and one from the Senate. Institutional rivalry did not permit a full merger of committee staff and these ar-rangements contributed significantly to the difficulties in building consensus and improving the joint committee's effectiveness.

Before the joint congressional committee got under way, President Reagan's commission of inquiry, chaired by former Senator John Tower, produced its report in February 1987.[11] It concluded that serious errors had been made, laws had been broken and there were major faults in the foreign policy-making process. It stopped short of accusing President Reagan of illegal conduct but found fault with almost all his senior staff and advisers. Tower concluded that 'The President's management style is to put the principal responsibility for policy review and implementa-tion on the shoulders of his advisers'[12] and 'Knowing his style, they should have been particularly mindful of the need for special attention to the manner in which this arms sales initiative developed and pro-ceeded'.[13] In particular, Tower spotlights Reagan's Chief of Staff, Don Regan, as especially culpable. According to Tower, Regan, 'as much as anyone, should have insisted that an orderly process be observed'.[14] Worse still, 'He must bear primary responsibility for the chaos that descended upon the White House'[15] when public disclosure occurred. But Regan was not alone in being criticized by the Tower Commission; virtually all the president's closest advisers and most senior officials, including National Security Advisers McFarlane and Poindexter, the Director of the CIA, Casey, and the Secretaries for State and Defense, Shultz and Weinberger, were accused of letting President Reagan down.

When an official report, commissioned by the president himself, condemns his senior staff in such critical terms, it is bound to provide substantial grist to the mill of scandal. But while the criticisms of cabinet members and other high officials were dramatic and devastating in themselves, the picture of Reagan's presidency painted by the report caused an even greater public and media reaction. It had long been recognized that Reagan was a broad-brush leader and not a micro-manager like his predecessor, Jimmy Carter. The Tower Commission depicted him as uncertain and distracted and, at times, 'the report makes the President sound like the inhabitant of a never-never land of imaginary policies'.[16] The image of the president conveyed in the press after the Tower Report was published suggested 'an almost pathetic figure – aloof, inattentive, unable to remember dates and details, manipulated by his subordinates, a remote and confused man'.[17]

The Tower Report eroded further the president's popularity. The dramatic slump after the November 1986 revelations of arms sales was given added impetus by the criticism of John Tower and his colleagues. A job-performance rating of 63 per cent in October 1986, had dropped to 47 per cent in December and to 40 per cent after the Tower Report in late February 1987.[18] The single but important consolation for the Reagan administration was that no one had suggested the president was a crook. The detachment which characterized his managerial style allowed Reagan to avoid personal culpability, to appear frank when he admitted mistakes had been made in the implementation of policy, and to sound credible when he pledged 'to get to the bottom of this matter'.[19]

By the time the joint congressional committee began eleven weeks of hearings in the summer of 1987, it was evident that President Reagan had survived the worst. There had already been a modest recovery in his approval ratings and the televized hearings provided key players in the Iran–Contra scandal with golden opportunities to justify their apparently outrageous conduct.

The majority of the joint committee (including three Republican Senators: Rudman, Cohen and Trible) concluded that 'the common ingredients of the Iran and Contra policies were secrecy, deception and disdain for the law'.[20] Senator Inouye, chairman of the joint committee, spoke of 'the privatization of American foreign policy'.[21] It identified initially the CIA and then the National Security Council as the source of the policy and its implementation. In particular, National Security Adviser Poindexter and NSC staff member Oliver North were cast in the role of reckless adventurers pursuing their own agendas without regard to the risks involved or the need to adhere to constitutional proprieties and legal niceties. But the majority did not excuse President Reagan. Their assessment was that Reagan was the author of the policy to sell arms secretly to Iran and also of the policy to maintain the Contras at any cost. The implementation of the programme was carried on without close supervision and they concluded that, if the president did not know what the staff of the National Security Council were doing, he should have done. They were unable to pinpoint exactly 'what the President knew and when he knew it', in the words of the famous Watergate question, because evidence had been destroyed, testimony was inconsistent and the president himself was forgetful. The majority report cited Reagan as first telling the Tower Board that he had approved the initial Israeli shipments of arms to Iran, later correcting himself by claiming that he had not and finally admitting that he could not remember whether he had or not.

The allegations against the administration were serious and emotive. Shipping arms to a nation which had been publicly identified by the United States as a promoter of terrorism was bad enough but to appear to trade the arms directly for the lives of American hostages was a blatant contradiction of stated American policy. If this was serious and politically embarrassing, the Contra dimension of the scandal suggested that the president had sought to bypass Congress by illegal and unconstitutional means. It further suggested that the means chosen themselves involved an illegal diversion of funds from arms sales to another country by a relatively junior member of the National Security Council staff, Oliver North, and it called into question whether President Reagan and the Secretaries of State and Defense approved or were even aware of such a dubious and high-risk foreign-policy manoeuvre.

The congressional hearings themselves revealed that the majority on the joint committee believed that the Iran–Contra scandal was a major and sustained attempt to deny Congress any role in the formulation and implementation of foreign policy. The view expressed by a number of administration officials was the opposite. In this view, the Iran–Contra scandal was a direct consequence of the usurpation by Congress of presidential prerogatives in foreign policy-making. While there may have been some mistakes or errors of judgement in the implementation of Reagan's policies, they arose because of the unwarranted and unjustified interference of Congress. It is a commonplace to note that the constitution is ambiguous on the question of who should direct American foreign policy. As Corwin noted, the constitution offers to the president and Congress 'an invitation to struggle' [22] in this area. The joint congressional hearings offered less a conclusive struggle for power and more a reluctant agreement to differ. As Foley has argued, Congress has no collective desire to run America's foreign policy but it does periodically like to reaffirm its right to participate and to be consulted.[23]

There were marked contrasts between the Watergate hearings and the Iran–Contra hearings. One of the most striking was the demeanour of the witnesses and especially the extraordinary testimony of Oliver North. While the Watergate witnesses were largely engaged in damage-limitation and blame-avoidance, Colonel North used the hearings to go on the offensive and to make his case to the committee and, more importantly, to the millions watching the proceedings at home on television. Once the Iran–Contra scandal had broken, it quickly became clear that North was a central figure. He had both orchestrated the arms sales to Iran and produced what he called 'the neat idea' of diverting the profits of the arm sales to help the Contras in Nicaragua. When Attorney-General Meese attempted to develop a coherent overview of what had happened, North began to shred documents and destroy computer records. It was clear to the Independent Counsel, Lawrence Walsh, not only that North was guilty of a variety of crimes but also that his prosecution could lead to the implication of more senior figures in the administration and perhaps even President Reagan himself. This was essentially the strategy used by prosecutors in Watergate when the threat of indictment encouraged White House staff and staff in the presidential campaign organization to implicate their superiors.

While it is not surprising that Congress asserted its right to hear North's testimony before criminal charges were laid, it is perhaps more remarkable that, in its overwhelming desire to put North in front of the committee and the cameras, Congress not only offered immunity to North but it was given on his terms. In May 1987, North's lawyer told the committee that his client would not give his immunized testimony privately before his public appearance. He claimed, with some legal ingenuity, that Congress was entitled to hear the testimony only once. When the Watergate witnesses appeared, the members of Congress and their legal staff knew what they were likely to say and were thus able to prepare lines of questioning, supplementary points and other elements necessary to a successful cross-examination. But in the case of North, the only people who knew what he was going to say were North himself and his lawyer.

Television is by definition a visual medium, and the image presented by Colonel North when he gave his first testimony before the joint congressional committee was striking and memorable. Although he had been on civilian duties with the National Security Council, North chose to wear his full dress uniform complete with his decorations for valour in the Vietnam War. His military bearing and his resolute manner helped support the view that here was an honest soldier doing his duty and obeying the orders of the president, his commander-in-chief.

Oliver North's testimony argued that it was within the power of the president 'to conduct secret activities to further the foreign policy goals of the United States' [24] and that this did not require sharing information with Congress. North was ready to admit that he had helped to prepare documents for Congress that were 'erroneous, misleading, evasive and wrong [25] but, despite these admissions, he was not prepared to concede the moral high ground to his congressional interrogators. Rather, he cloaked his behaviour in military camouflage and represented himself as serving higher policy goals. In a comment calculated to emphasize that those at the sharp end of covert military activity have to make decisions on a different moral level, he observed 'we all had to weigh in the balance the difference between lives and lies'.[26] The committee's decision to accept North's terms for giving his testimony meant that it 'publicly and blindly examined a hostile, articulate and immunized witness without the protection and guidance of a significant prior statement'.[27] With his sense of theatre and occasion, Oliver North took full advantage of his opportunities and, to a substantial body of American public opinion, North appeared, if not exactly a hero, then the scapegoat for the incompetence, wrongdoing or negligence of his superiors.

President Harry Truman had a sign on his desk reading, 'the buck stops here'. In the congressional Iran–Contra hearing, the buck stopped with Admiral John Poindexter. Like his subordinate, Oliver North, Poindexter enjoyed immunity from prosecution for anything he said. In his testimony, Poindexter went out of his way to protect President Reagan by accepting responsibility for Iran–Contra. When John Dean had felt the sword of Watergate on him, he turned it against President Nixon. In sharp contrast, Poindexter was prepared to fall on the Iran–Contra sword. He claimed that, unlike Watergate, there was no 'smoking gun' because he had deliberately withheld crucial information from

KING ALFRED'S COLLEGE
LIBRARY

President Reagan. It should perhaps be noted that Poindexter's penchant for self-sacrifice was both temporary and limited and, when he was subsequently tried in 1990 for a number of alleged offences, he was keen to point out he was not personally responsible for the Iran–Contra scandal and that his actions were authorized by President Reagan. Poindexter's convictions were quashed on appeal in 1991 because it had not been shown to the extent the court required that his widely publicized immunized congressional testimony did not affect the testimony of witnesses against him.

The members of the joint congressional committee did not achieve the fame or respect enjoyed by the Ervin Committee during Watergate. There were no new dramatic revelations and most of the facts had been put together either by Attorney-General Meese or by the Tower Commission some months earlier. Oliver North's bravura performance had stolen the headlines and wrested the initiative and the spotlight away from Congress. These were congressional hearings yet Congress did not seem fully in control of its own agenda. The hunt for the 'smoking gun' which would imperil the presidency of Ronald Reagan was frustrated partly because no gun could be found and partly because of the refusal of the good soldiers, North and Poindexter, to incriminate their commander-in-chief. The committee was deprived of another potential star witness when CIA Director, Bill Casey, died on 6 May 1987, the day after Congress began its public hearings on the Iran–Contra scandal.

The instigator of the arms sales to Iran was dead, North had been sacked, Poindexter had resigned and, the American public now knew what many had long suspected, that President Reagan rarely bothered to find out what his subordinates did after he gave them vague and general instructions. But at least there was the consolation that this president was a well-meaning man who was attempting to achieve some important foreign-policy goals. Satirists could turn Howard Baker's famous Watergate questions, 'what did the president know and when did he know it?', into 'did the president know anything and when did he forget it?' But the fact remained that the president was pursuing policy aims that enjoyed wide public support.

As a scandal, Iran–Contra began to run out of steam after North's testimony to Congress. There seemed little public or press appetite for an intensive consideration of the respective foreign-policy roles of Congress and the president. It seems almost that having established both that the president was not a crook engaged in a criminal conspiracy and that there was no prospect of impeachment, the scandal lost impetus and direction. The joint committee failed to produce a unanimous report and the gulf between the majority and minority reports was so wide that it was difficult to believe they were addressing the same scandal. All six House Republican members and two Senate Republicans voted against the majority report and their chief spokesman, Senator Orrin Hatch, argued that it reached 'hysterical conclusions' and reads 'as if it were a weapon in the guerrilla warfare' [28] between Congress and the White House. The minority report was leaked to the *New York Times* the day before official publication in an attempt to draw attention away from the majority report.

The majority report's conclusions and recommendations were not headline-grabbing or likely to arouse keen public interest and concern. It found that the Iran–Contra scandal occurred because of the deficiencies of individuals and not as a result of deficiencies in the law or the system of governance. Even the Chairman, Senator Inouye, described their recommendations as 'modest' and his House equivalent Lee Hamilton, offered the optimistic observation that 'Congress and the President must work together in an atmosphere of mutual respect and trust'.[29] One magazine noted that 'after a day of obligatory headlines, news of the report vanished as abruptly as an April snowfall', and it characterized the report's conclusion as expressing 'the hope that the next time the White House sets out to violate the law it will inform the Congress of its travel plans'.[30]

After the televised hearings and the congressional report, the Iran–Contra scandal lost its high-profile coverage but it continued to splutter intermittently into life through the work of the Independent Counsel, Lawrence Walsh. It lurked just below the surface of the 1988 presidential election with allegations about George Bush's knowledge and involvement in the arms sales to Iran and diversion of the proceeds to the Contras in Nicaragua. Bush was a former Director of the CIA but kept insisting that he was 'out of the loop' and did not attend the crucial meetings. The inconsistencies and improbabilities in his account of his role provoked some public scepticism about whether he was telling the whole truth.

When Reagan left office he did so on the crest of a renewed if modest wave of popularity engendered by his meetings with Gorbachev and the signing of a disarmament treaty. His reputation and popularity were never restored to their first-term heights but neither did he leave office in disgrace as Nixon had done. But his departure did not end the Iran—Contra scandal as a factor in American politics. The Independent Counsel, Lawrence Walsh, brought indictments and secured convictions against many of those most intimately involved in the scandal, including North and Poindexter. But their convictions were overturned on appeal in 1991. Republicans in Congress, and President Bush himself, sought to create an alternative scandal by alleging biased behaviour by Walsh. Bush's view was that Walsh was enquiring into a political, rather than a legal, dispute between a Republican Administration and a Democratic Congress over foreign policy. In this view, the real issues involved not the infractions of laws but the contravention of government policies. Bush argued that 'An attempt to criminalize public policy differences jeopardizes any President's ability to govern. By seeking to craft criminal violations from a political foreign policy dispute, the Office of Independent Counsel was cast in a biased position from the beginning'.[31] President Bush was in a position to act on this conviction and, when Walsh belatedly brought charges against former Secretary of Defense, Casper Weinberger, Bush pardoned Weinberger.

The last flickers of the scandal were evident when, almost seven years after his appointment, Lawrence Walsh's final report was published on 18 January 1994.[32] As virtually all the major players in the Iran—Contra drama, Reagan, Bush, Meese, Poindexter, McFarlane, Regan, Casey and North, had left the public stage, the media and public reactions were muted and mixed. It all seemed long ago, the Ayatollah Khomeini was dead and the Sandinistas were no longer in power in Nicaragua. Despite Walsh's prolonged efforts, there were no serious criminal convictions and no exemplary punishments. More importantly, there have been no major institutional, legal or procedural reforms aimed at reducing the likelihood or minimizing the consequences of a similar scandal in the future. If the institutional and policy issues raised by Iran—Contra went unexamined, the political imperative seemed to be not so much bringing the presidency under control but reining in independent counsels. Perhaps the ultimate irony of the Iran—Contra scandal is that the only concerted political response was the decision of Congress to allow the independent counsel legislation to lapse. This was to have implications for the Whitewater scandal discussed later in this book.

Watergate and Iran–Contra: Analogies, Metaphors and Political Lessons

There are obvious and striking parallels between the Watergate and the Iran–Contra scandals. Both arose in the context of overseas conflicts which had proved difficult for the United States to resolve. If Vietnam demonstrated that there were, after all, limits to American power, Iran and Nicaragua revealed how tight those limits were. The United States seemed powerless to prevent the overthrow of pro-American regimes and their replacement by regimes hostile to American commercial, political and security interests. President Nixon made his political reputation as a Cold War warrior and by condemning his Democratic opponents as being 'soft' on communism. Given his political pedigree, it is perhaps not surprising that his first instincts on gaining the White House were to extend without congressional approval, and, if possible, win the Vietnam War. But he felt inhibited and frustrated by the increasingly vocal anti-war sentiment at home and what he took to be the disloyalty of officials working for the government. The leaking of the *Pentagon Papers* by Daniel Ellsberg was a major factor in the creation of the Plumbers' unit and the subsequent burglaries of the Watergate building. In Nixon's view, he was forced to overcome domestic political opposition in order to fulfil the global mission of the United States as protector of the free world.

While there are obvious personality, character and intellectual differences between Richard Nixon and Ronald Reagan, there were also important similarities. Both were Republicans elected to succeed Democrats and they faced Democratic Congresses for all or part of their administrations. Ronald Reagan was also elected as a candidate with a more aggressive stance toward the Soviet Union. His message to the American people was that Carter's weakness had led to the Iranian hostage crisis, the Soviet invasion of Afghanistan and the spread of communist subversion in central America in general and El Salvador and Nicaragua in particular. Once in office, Reagan was determined to live up to his campaign rhetoric and he sought to reassert America's standing in the world. Cuba had long been a particular source of frustration, and preventing the extension of Cuban-style communism in Central America was a main concern of his presidency. But the shadow of Vietnam continued to influence media, public and congressional opinion, and Reagan became increasingly unhappy about the criticisms of his Central American policies and what he saw as the obstruction of Congress.

In the case of Iran, Reagan had profited from Carter's inability to release the US Embassy hostages[33] and, faced with a new spurt in hostage-taking by Iranian-backed elements in the Lebanon, he was anxious, for both political and humanitarian reasons, to do all in his power to secure their release. The death of more than 200 American military personnel from a terrorist bombing in Beirut convinced Reagan that the hostage crisis could not be resolved by the use of American force. To exercise leverage on the hostage-takers, he had to reach and to influence their paymasters and sponsors in Tehran. Reagan believed his policies toward Iran and Nicaragua were morally and politically correct and he rejected the counsel of his critics that he should engage in quiet diplomacy. Quiet diplomacy had not freed the Embassy hostages, deterred the Soviets from invading Afghanistan or prevented the Sandinistas from supporting their comrades in El Salvador. But his domestic opponents had free access to the media as well as majorities in Congress and, whatever action the United States took, it would have to be by covert means. What the public did not know, they could not complain about. They supported his policy aims and it was his responsibility to ensure that these aims were realized. Similarly, if Congress would not co-operate, it would have to be bypassed.

The prohibition of the Boland Amendments impelled the Reagan Administration to solicit donations from other countries, notably Saudi Arabia and Brunei, to help the Contras. The lack of congressionally authorized funds prompted North's 'neat idea' of taking the Iran arms sales profits and diverting them to the Contras. The initial sale of arms to Iran was conducted through Israel to disguise the real connection between the United States and Iran. Such transactions necessarily involved third parties, not all of whom were entirely trustworthy, as well as an element of deception and covering of tracks. Similarly, the Watergate burglaries conducted by the Plumbers' unit were financed from campaign contributions amassed by the Committee to Re-elect the President. Many of these contributions were illegal and the funds have never been properly accounted for. Thus, the use of private or illicit funds to support presidential policies is an important common feature of these scandals.

Those entrusted with the implementation of covert operations are often people with somewhat unconventional careers. They frequently come from military or intelligence backgrounds and they are people used to obeying orders, to operating on 'a need to know basis' and familiar with the notion of 'plausible deniability'. They tend to place great weight on the authority of the president as commander-in-chief and tend not to be overly sensitive to issues of democratic accountability, legal due process and the public right to know. In Watergate, the key action men were G. Gordon Liddy and E. Howard Hunt. The former was an ex-FBI man and the latter was ex-CIA. Liddy, in particular, showed great dedication to the cause and loyalty to his political masters, CRP Director, John Mitchell and President Nixon. He was once described as 'a knight looking for a liege lord to serve'.[34] Liddy not only offered to take all the blame for Watergate but, at one time, even offered himself as an assassination victim.[35] Hunt used his prior involvement in the abortive Bay of Pigs operation to recruit his former associates, the Miami-based Cubans, as part of the Watergate burglary team. There seems some evidence that they believed they were being recruited for another CIA operation. Neither Liddy nor Hunt ever expressed the slightest hesitation in carrying out their orders. When eventually tried, Liddy declined to say anything and this refusal was maintained even in the face of the threat of a heavy prison sentence. Liddy spoke publicly about the Watergate burglary only after the statute of limitations expired in 1980.

Lt-Col. Oliver North, who worked on the National Security Council staff, is credited with initiating the bold and successful plan to capture the hijackers of the *Achille Lauro*. A former Vietnam veteran, decorated for bravery, North had acquired a reputation as a man impatient with constraints who could get things done and who was not afraid of doing the dirty work. Unquestioning in his loyalty and convinced in the righteousness of his cause, North was determined to combat the evil of communism in Nicaragua by any means at his disposal. The need for 'action officers' in covert operations is obvious, but Iran–Contra and Watergate reveal the political dangers of delegating authority to individuals as eccentric, imprudent and zealous as North and Liddy.

There was a significant continuity of personnel from Watergate to Iran–Contra in the administration, in Congress and in the news media. Senator Howard Baker, the ranking Republican on the Ervin Committee during Watergate, became President Reagan's chief of staff after the critical Tower Commission report made the position of chief of staff, Donald Regan, untenable. Pat Buchanan, a speechwriter for Nixon and a loyal stalwart in his last days in office, later became communications director in the Reagan White House. Larry Speakes, Reagan's press secretary, had worked for James St Clair, Nixon's defence attorney during Watergate.

Senator Inouye, the chairman of the Iran–Contra committee, had been a member of the Ervin Committee. Senators William Cohen and Paul Sarbanes, who served on the Iran–Contra committee, had also served on the House Judiciary Committee during Watergate and had voted to impeach President Nixon. Congressmen Jack Brook and Peter Rodino also served on both committees and had also voted to impeach Nixon. In the media, the former Watergate prosecutors, Cox and Jaworski, and Watergate felons, John Erlichman and John Dean, became pundits and commentators on the unfolding Iran–Contra scandal.

But the links between Watergate and Iran–Contra extended well beyond continuities in personnel.[36] They influenced the ways in which the administration responded to the revelation of the scandal, the nature and form of the congressional response, the coverage and interpretation of the scandal by the media, the legal framework, the mechanisms of investigation and prosecution, and the public understanding of the scandal and its importance.

Although President Reagan's first instinct seemed to be to deny there was an arms-for-hostages deal [37] and to hope the matter would go away, his senior advisers in the White House were determined not to go down the Watergate road of stonewall defence. Theodore Draper suggests that Attorney-General Meese and other staff were 'haunted' by the Watergate cover-up and were 'determined at all costs to avoid a repetition'.[38] In one of the many ironies of Iran–Contra, a cover-up is exactly what Independent Counsel, Laurence Walsh, charged Meese with in his *Final Report*. But no legal charges were ever brought against Meese and, in response to the *Final Report*'s judgement, Meese's attorney observed that the most important question raised by it is why did Walsh 'so abuse his public trust and dishonor his appointment by issuing a document filled with distortions of fact, misuse of evidence, and false accusations against honorable public officials who are totally innocent of any wrongdoing'?[39]

In Watergate, there was a gradual process of erosion as the lower ranks were arrested, charged and plea bargained, and the tide of suspicion rose higher and higher through the ranks of the White House staff. Haldeman and Erlichman stuck it out for ten months before resigning and Nixon waited eleven months before agreeing to appoint an outside prosecutor. The Iran–Contra approach was very different. Within three weeks of the original revelations, Poindexter and North had gone, and three weeks later an independent counsel was appointed to investigate the scandal. Arriving seven years later and unsupported by legal convictions or even charges, Walsh's assertions of a cover-up are perhaps beside the point. What is clear is that the Reagan administration sought to behave very differently from the Nixon administration's conduct in the first months of Watergate.

One study of media responses to Iran–Contra suggests that there was a heavy reliance on analogies with Watergate.[40] But, whereas Woodward and Bernstein can claim some credit for helping to unravel the Watergate scandal, the Iran–Contra story was handed to the press corps by the White House. When faced with a story as big as Iran–Contra, journalists began to look for a lexicon or guide to help make sense of these complex events and situations. Liberal and conservative journalists alike invoked Watergate to help make sense of Iran–Contra. They could anticipate congressional inquiries and special prosecutors, and they could compare North to Liddy, Meese to Mitchell and Reagan to Nixon. Even when it was acknowledged that there were substantial differences between the scandals, the analogies were still drawn.

When the story of the arms shipments first broke in November 1986, the first press reaction was that this was another example of American incompetence in foreign policy. But when President Reagan's first denials of an arms-for-hostages deal began to crumble in the face of the evidence, the press began to focus on the president himself. The reporters started asking questions about presidential guilt, presidential ignorance and presidential credibility.

The reiteration of Baker's Watergate question, 'what did the president know and when did he know it?', provided some protection for Reagan. In the absence of a 'smoking gun', positive proof of the orchestration of a criminal conspiracy, Reagan's fate was unlikely to be as bad as Nixon's. Reagan had not pursued his Iranian or Nicaraguan policies from a position of narrow self-interest but in furtherance of humanitarian concerns and his perception of vital national interests.

The Reagan Administration's disclosures, its ordering of investigations and the president's apparent openness all served to deflect attention away from criticism of the actions and policies themselves. The issues of how many lives were lost and the political repercussions and consequences of Reagan's Iran—Contra policies were never seriously explored. The verdict of well-intentioned but ill-judged and incompetently executed seemed more appropriate than judgements of a criminal, conspiratorial or unconstitutional nature. The media focused more on presidential credibility, trust and popularity than on the alleged 'privatization of American foreign policy'.

If the experience and trauma of Watergate influenced the ways in which both politicians and the public viewed Iran—Contra, the key issues of cover-up and conspiracy had been successfully addressed by the departure of North and Poindexter and the administration's apparent desire to 'get to the bottom' of what happened. The narrowing of the issue to one of criminal conduct helped both to defuse wider concerns about the foreign policy-making process and to protect Reagan from the possibility of impeachment. Just as the impeachment articles approved by the House Judiciary Committee in Watergate excluded those related to the conduct of foreign policy, there was no political interest in seeking an impeachment of Reagan on grounds of improper or unconstitutional actions in his policies toward Iran or Central America. The inconsistencies and ambiguities of the congressional approach to supporting the Contras weakened the Iran—Contra committee's ability or desire to take the moral and constitutional high ground. The failure of the committee to establish whether or not Reagan had prior knowledge of the diversion of funds served to confirm that impeachment was not on the congressional agenda.

Majority public opinion saw Iran—Contra as at least as serious as Watergate.[41] Nearly half those polled thought Reagan was lying about his knowledge of the diversion of funds. A large majority believed that there had been a cover-up. These expressions of public opinion probably tended to encourage the media, Congress and the independent counsel to pursue their inquiries vigorously. But the analogies with Watergate served, from one perspective, to generate a mistaken interpretation of the scandal. As Schudson notes, 'Watergate was invoked for rhetorical purposes; calling Iran—Contra "worse than Watergate" was a way to demand attention'.[42] Once the 'smoking gun' question had been answered in the negative, the media tended to lose interest. If there was to be no possibility of impeachment, the scandal lost momentum and focus. The issues were complex and confusing and the policy lessons were unclear.

Public and media opinion did force President Reagan to restructure his personal staff in the White House, and his public-approval ratings never fully recovered from the revelations of the Iran–Contra scandal.[43] His scope for subsequent policy initiatives was severely circumscribed and it has been argued that Reagan's post-Iran–Contra initiatives were those that 'coincided with the agenda of his liberal opponents'.[44] The 'lame duck' character of his last years in office were accentuated by the fall in his public standing occasioned by the Iran–Contra scandal. The Tower Commission, the joint congressional committee and the independent counsel demonstrated that President Reagan was 'actively culpable and passively negligent'[45] in his handling of these foreign-policy initiatives. The public and media understood both that the policies were his policies and that Reagan did not know or did not want to know about their implementation. Conversely, a key problem for Nixon during Watergate was that his denials of prior and subsequent knowledge lacked plausibility.

Watergate was traumatic and many of the participants and spectators in Iran–Contra were anxious to avoid a repetition. These anxieties caused them to refrain from mention of impeachment, from claiming executive privilege and from comparing Reagan to Nixon. Thus, although analogies were drawn with Watergate, the lessons drawn from that scandal meant that Iran–Contra unravelled more quickly and more comprehensively. Although the full facts of Iran–Contra may never be known because of the secrecy of third countries and the shredding activities of North and others, the essential facts were revealed by Attorney-General Meese within weeks of the first revelation, and they were confirmed and amplified by the president's own board of inquiry, the Tower Commission, a few months later. Despite the delay of the independent counsel, this was no 'long national nightmare'. In effect, the Iran–Contra scandal was over as a national event when the congressional hearings concluded. The trials, convictions and subsequent successful appeals of North and Poindexter were sideshows. The independent counsel struggled on but a line was drawn under Iran–Contra when, on Christmas Eve, 1992, President Bush, having already been defeated in the presidential election by Bill Clinton, pardoned the former Secretary of Defense, Weinberger, just two weeks before his Iran–Contra-related trial was due to begin.

In the view of Lawrence Walsh, the ultimate scandals of Iran–Contra were the decisions of Congress to give North and Poindexter immunity in exchange for testimony and the Reagan Administration's refusal to declassify intelligence information necessary to the trials of North and Poindexter. Absent these decisions, and the outcome for President Reagan and his senior staff may have been very different. The final irony of Iran–Contra is, perhaps, that what is often portrayed as a struggle for authority and power between the president and Congress culminated in both the executive and legislative branches using their power to prevent a judicially appointed official from successfully prosecuting those responsible for the Iran–Contra scandal. Lawrence Walsh may not have been the victim of a Watergate-style, 'Saturday Night Massacre', but there is no doubt that, between them, the White House and Capitol Hill made his task virtually impossible.

Conclusion

The responsibility for the Iran–Contra scandal is a shared one. While President Reagan is criticized for his inattention and detached management style, his senior cabinet officers, Shultz and Weinberger are blamed for not doing more to monitor, amend or reverse a foreign-policy initiative they regarded as dangerous and probably illegal. Don Regan is condemned for not compensating for Reagan's management deficiencies, and Attorney-General Meese has been criticized for not assembling all the facts in due time. George Bush has been criticized for not being frank about his own knowledge and involvement. CIA Director Casey was chastized for attempting to run his own foreign policy, and National Security Advisers, McFarlane and Poindexter, have been condemned for using the National Security Council as an operational rather than an advisory body. They have also been criticised for being overzealous and for operating without regard to legality and proper authority.

If the executive branch has come in for wholesale criticism from the legislative branch, some observers point to the failure of Congress to perform responsibly its oversight functions. The activist role played by the Senate in the 1970s gave way to a Republican majority in 1981 and five years of senatorial deference. As Bailey notes, 'By failing to challenge other aspects of Reagan's foreign policy, the Senate facilitated the growth of a complacent attitude within the Administration which ultimately led to measures such as the arms sales to Iran and the diversion of funds to the Contras. In a more challenging environment, ... it is unlikely that either of these measure would have been implemented'.[46] Where the Senate did intervene on the issue of aid to the Contras, it did so in an inconsistent and ambiguous fashion.

If the details of the Iran–Contra scandal were too complex for most Americans to follow, the broad outlines were clear. The story of presidential deception, of secrecy and of cover-up was easy to grasp and easy to report. The scandal had an impact not only on Reagan's reputation for honesty and competence but also on the reputation of his successor, George Bush. 'What did the president know and when did he know it?' was enshrined as the scandal question in American politics, and variations on it have been posed in relation to Whitewater and other scandals of the Clinton Administration.

To the many who are suspicious of executive power, Iran–Contra was no more an aberration than Watergate. Many American presidents have been so frustrated by the constraints they experience that they succumb to the temptation of bold initiatives, of decisive, dramatic action that will solve apparently intractable problems. In the foreign-policy arena, the opportunities are greatest. The Reagan Presidency was characterized by a number of such schemes: the invasion of Grenada; the *Achille Lauro* rescue; and the bombing of Libya. But effective policy short-cuts are rare, and Iran–Contra is a classic example of what happens when things go wrong. The principals in Watergate either went to jail or were disgraced; the principals in Iran–Contra largely escaped such indignities. But if the scandal of Watergate disgraced the Nixon Administration, the scandal of Iran–Contra served both to discredit the Reagan Administration and to erode further public confidence in American government.

Notes

1. The official title is assistant to the President for national security affairs but the post-holder is normally referred to as the national security adviser.
2. The CIA had already concluded that information previously supplied by Ghorbanifar was not only wrong but had been intentionally fabricated. See Bob Woodward, *Veil: The Secret Wars of the CIA* (London: Headline Book Publishing, 1987), pp. 511–12.
3. Quoted in Theodore Draper, 'The fall of Reagan's Junta', *New York Review of Books*, 22 October 1987, p. 50.
4. For a useful discussion of the Boland Amendments, see Michael Foley, *Mumbling Across the Branches*, Aberystwyth, International Politics Research Papers, No. 6, pp. 6–14.
5. The weakness of this claim is illustrated by the fact that support was given to Contra leader, Eden Pastora, who operated from Costa Rica which is south of Nicaragua. El Salvador is to the north of Nicaragua. See Woodward, pp. 238–9.
6. Foley, p. 9.
7. Senator Goldwater summarized his feelings in the following words: 'It gets down

to one, little, simple phrase: I am pissed off', and he continued: 'this is no way to run a railroad and I find myself in a hell of a quandary ... The President has asked us to back his foreign policy. Bill, how can we back his foreign policy when we don't know what the hell he is doing?', *Congressional Quarterly Weekly Report*, 14 April 1984, p. 833.

8. Foley, p. 11.

9. Foley, pp. 11–12.

10. Special prosecutors are appointed and can be removed by the Attorney-General as the Cox case demonstrated. Independent counsels are appointed by a division of the Federal Court of Appeal at the request of the Attorney-General. The reality is that the Attorney-General can neither choose which individual is appointed nor remove that individual from office. The post of independent counsel replaced that of special prosecutor as part of a 1983 amendment to the Ethics in Government Act, 1978, PL 95–521.

11. The Tower Commission Report (official title, President's Special Review Board, Washington D.C., Government Printing Office, 26 February 1987).

12. Tower, p. 79.

13. Tower, p. 80.

14. Tower, p. 81.

15. Tower, p. 81.

16. R. W. Apple in Introduction to Tower, p. xiii.

17. David Ignatius and Michael Getler, 'This Isn't Watergate, But the Moral Is the Same', *Washington Post*, 1 March 1987.

18. Gallup Poll press release, 28 February 1988.

19. Quoted by Michael Cornfield and David Alistair Yalof, 'Innocent by reason of analogy: How the Watergate analogy served both Reagan and the press during the Iran–Contra affair', *Corruption and Reform*, vol. 3, No. 2, 1988, p. 197. The quotation is taken from a television address, 2 December 1986, and the commitment was repeated in President Reagan's State of the Union address, 27 January 1987.

20. *Report of the Congressional Committee Investigating the Iran–Contra Affair*, with Supplemental, Minority and Additional Views, Washington D.C., Government Printing Office, 17 November 1987, p. 11. The majority and minority reports are analyzed in Robert Williams, 'Presidential power and the abuse of office: The case of the Iran–Contra affair', *Corruption and Reform*, vol. 3, No. 2, 1988, pp. 171–83.

21. Quoted in M. Shaw (ed.), *Roosevelt to Reagan: The Development of the Modern Presidency* (London: C. Hurst and Company, 1987), p. 309.

22. E. Corwin, *The President: Office and Powers* (New York, 1940), p. 200.

23. Michael Foley, 'Congress and policy-making: can it cope with foreign affairs?', in Robert Williams (ed.), *Explaining American Politics: Issues and Interpretations* (London: Routledge, 1990), pp. 91–2.

24. Testimony to Iran–Contra Committees, 13 July 1987, quoted in Louis Fisher, 'The foundations of a scandal', *Corruption and Reform*, vol. 3, No. 2, 1988, p. 158.

25. Testimony, 8 July 1987, quoted in Fisher, p. 161.

26. Testimony, 8 July 1987, quoted in Fisher, p. 161.

27. *Final Report of the Independent Counsel for Iran–Contra Matters*, US Court of Appeal for the District of Columbia Circuit, Division for the Purpose of Appointing Independent Counsel, Division No. 86–6, 1994, Volume 1, p. 35. Hereafter cited as Final Report.

28. *The Guardian*, 18 November 1987.

29. *International Herald Tribune*, 20 November 1987.

30. *Harper's Magazine*, February, 1988, p. 46.

31. *Final Report*, vol. III, p. 21.

32. The *Final Report* is analyzed in Robert Williams, 'The last word on the Iran–Contra Affair?', *Crime, Law and Social Change*, vol. 23, 1995, pp. 367–85.

33. One account suggests that members of the Reagan–Bush campaign worked to delay the release of the hostages in Iran to damage President Carter's prospects of re-election. See Gary Sick, *October Surprise: America's Hostages in Iran and the Election of Ronald Reagan* (London: I. B. Tauris and Co., 1991).

34. Fred Emery, *Watergate: The Corruption and Fall of Richard Nixon* (London: Jonathan Cape, 1994), p. 56.

35. Emery, pp. 164–5.

36. There is a perceptive discussion of the connections between Watergate and Iran–Contra in Michael Schudson, *Watergate in American Memory* (New York: Basic Books, 1992), pp. 165–84.

37. Lou Cannon, *President Reagan: The Role of a Lifetime* (New York: Simon and Schuster, 1991), p. 680.

38. Theodore Draper, *A Very Thin Line: The Iran–Contra Affairs* (New York: Hill and Wang, 1991), p. 522.

39. *Final Report*, vol. 3, p. 406.

40. Cornfield and Yalof, pp. 185–206.

41. Polls cited in Schudson, p. 171. He also makes the interesting point that no one seems to have argued that Watergate raised more serious constitutional issues than Iran–Contra. He points out that there are grounds for arguing that Iran–Contra, unlike Watergate, did not involve a criminal conspiracy. Schudson, p. 260.

42. Schudson, p. 260.

43. In October 1986 his Gallup poll rating of 'job performance' was 63 per cent, it fell to 40 per cent in February 1987 and never rose higher than 54 per cent until December 1988. See Schudson, p. 173.

44. Benjamin Ginsberg and Martin Shefter, *Politics By Other Means: The Declining Importance of Elections in America* (New York: Basic Books, 1990), p. 148.

45. Schudson, p. 181.

46. Christopher J. Bailey, 'President Reagan, the U.S. Senate, and American Foreign Policy, 1981–1986', *Journal of American Studies*, vol. 21, No. 2, August 1987, pp. 180–1.

CHAPTER 4

Whitewater

The Whitewater scandal has its origins in events that occurred long before Bill Clinton was elected to the White House and even before he became Governor of Arkansas in 1979. In one sense the story is very simple. The charges made against Bill and Hillary Clinton are that they used their political connections in Arkansas to try to make some easy money, that Bill Clinton exploited his position as governor to obstruct inquiries into the financial conduct of his business partners and that, once in the White House, attempts were made to cover up the role played by the Clintons in the land deal. It is alleged that, in pursuit of these aims, the Clintons have lied about their involvement, have with-held evidence and have sought to obstruct police, congressional and independent counsel inquiries.

In another sense, the Whitewater scandal is infinitely complex. Understanding its full implications requires an understanding of state and federal bank, savings and loan and tax regulations as well as cam-paign finance law. It involves understanding the processes of federal investigations and the billing practices of law firms. It demands a fam-iliarity with the death of White House Counsel, Vincent Foster, and an understanding of police procedures and jurisdictions as well as forensic and ballistic evidence. It requires a grasp of congressional forms of inquiry and of the role and functions of independent counsels. It demands knowledge of sundry associated scandals including the savings and loan failures, Hillary Clinton's commodity speculations, the activ-ities of James and Susan McDougal, David Hale, Webster Hubbell, Margaret Williams and a lengthy cast of other characters. In short, any account of Whitewater is bound to be inadequate and limited.[1] The Senate Special Committee on Whitewater produced a report in July 1996 which ran to more than 1,000 pages, but its judgements are questionable, and many issues were unresolved and remain contested.

Despite its formidable complexity, Whitewater offers a fascinating example of how modern scandals develop, how they are sustained and how they proliferate. The account offered here attempts to identify the structure of the scandal without delving into the fine detail and without exploring the more lurid accounts found on the internet. A Whitewater conspiracy literature of the 'Did Elvis Assassinate JFK?' variety has developed, and the ways in which extreme interpretations of political events gain mainstream coverage will be discussed later in this chapter.

What is not in dispute is that Bill and Hillary Clinton became partners in the Whitewater Development Corporation with their friends, James and Susan McDougal, in 1979. The plan was to buy some land and develop it. Bill Clinton was elected Governor of Arkansas later in 1979 and, on most accounts, subsequently played a relatively passive role in the venture. The financing of the Whitewater investment is unclear but it seems that the Clintons and McDougals believed they would share equally any profits. The Clintons' consistent story is that they were 'passive investors' and that the McDougals managed and operated the Whitewater Development Corporation. In succeeding years, McDougal acquired interests in a bank and in the Madison Guaranty Savings and Loan Association (Madison). The affairs of Madison, the bank and Whitewater were to become confusingly intermingled. The Whitewater venture was not a success and various loans at a number of banks were required to keep the investment afloat. At the same time, Mrs Clinton, in her capacity as a partner in the Rose Law Firm, undertook legal work for McDougal's business ventures. McDougal got into serious business difficulties and, dissatisfied with his handling of events, Mrs Clinton took control of the Whitewater Development Company in 1988 and remained in charge until 1992 when the Clintons sold their share to McDougal for $1,000.

In 1989, the Madison Savings and Loan went bust leaving the tax-payers with a bill of approximately $60 million. It was McDougal's business failure that subsequently made the Clintons' Whitewater link to McDougal seem questionable and which gave the first glimmer of a 'proto-scandal' in the presidential election campaign in 1992. An article by Jeff Gerth appeared in the *New York Times*, headlined 'Clintons Joined S & L Operator in an Ozark Real-Estate Venture'.[2] The article reported the ties between the McDougals and Clintons, questioned tax deductions relating to the Whitewater investment made by the Clintons, and suggested that Whitewater may have been used as a conduit to funnel money either for the 'Clintons' own use or for Bill Clinton's election campaigns'.[3]

Anticipating the article and concerned about future media interest, the Clinton campaign organized their response. A Colorado lawyer, James Lyons, a friend and supporter of the Clintons, was asked to review the documentation. He subsequently called in an accounting firm to help in reconstructing the financial history. The Lyons Report concluded that, far from making money out of Whitewater, the Clintons had lost some $70,000. The obvious political message was that, if the Clintons were supposed to be benefiting financially from their political position in Arkansas, it was certainly not through Whitewater.

The Whitewater 'proto-scandal' had been temporarily defused and it did not develop into a significant issue in the 1992 presidential election campaign. Savings and Loans had been collapsing all around the country, and the involvement of President Bush's son in one of the more spectacular failures discouraged the Republicans from making an issue of the McDougal/Clinton connection. In any event, the apparent loss suffered by the Clintons meant that it was difficult to suggest any form of corruption.

But within the Resolution Trust Corporation (RTC: the body responsible for sorting out the Savings and Loan mess), a criminal investigator, L. Jean Lewis, began to take a keen interest in the allegations made in the *New York Times* article. Madison was on her list of savings and loans to investigate but had been given a low priority. Lewis now set aside her original priority cases, including Savings and Loans with losses of almost a billion dollars, in order to concentrate on Jim McDougal's Madison. She has denied that this had anything to do with her own strong conservative views but an FBI agent later testified that Lewis had told him she was going to 'alter history'[4] by completing a criminal referral before the presidential election. Lewis's opinion of Bill Clinton was revealed in a letter to a friend written in February 1992, in which she described Clinton as 'a lying bastard'.[5]

After making the criminal referral, it seems that Lewis tried repeatedly to get the US Attorney's Office in Little Rock to act on it before the election. The Republican US Attorney, Charles Banks, did not respond to the referral before the election and it was not until October 1993 that his Democrat successor formally declined to act on the referral. Banks was of the view that Lewis's insistence on urgency suggested an attempt to intervene in the presidential election. But Lewis was not easily deterred and continued to focus her efforts on Madison despite the consequent neglect of much larger cases. In Lewis's view, the attempts to divert her from Madison and to subject her referral to legal review in the Justice Department were suggestive of deliberate obstruction. To Republicans, Lewis was later to be characterized as the courageous heroine of the Whitewater scandal. To many others she seemed obsessive and motivated by a political animus against Bill and Hillary Clinton.

The Republicans were interested in uncovering President Clinton's past because they were convinced, in the light of the Gennifer Flowers scandal, that other skeletons would be uncovered. They suspected that in a small state like Arkansas a degree of political incest was inevitable and that the small political elite would act as a mutual aid society. Whitewater was a side issue compared to the Savings and Loan scandal and there was speculation about an exchange of favours between McDougal and Clinton. In particular, there was interest in discovering whether Clinton had received illegal campaign contributions channelled by McDougal and whether the Clintons were being subsidized by McDougal in exchange for political and regulatory protection.

One of the striking features of the Whitewater scandal is that there is no single, unbroken narrative. Rather, there is a number of side scandals which deflect the path of inquiry. The most obvious of these was the death of Deputy White House Counsel, Vincent Foster, in July 1993. Foster was a long time friend of the Clintons and had previously been a partner with Hillary Clinton in the Rose Law Firm in Little Rock. The circumstances of Foster's death have given rise to much speculation and suspicion.[6] At the time of his death, Foster was a key adviser to the Clintons on Whitewater and on yet another side scandal, Travelgate, and it was reasonable to assume that his office contained documents relevant to these two issues.

Foster's death had all the appearance of a suicide but there was no note near his body in Fort Marcy Park and no note was found in his home. On the night of Foster's death, a number of White House staff entered Foster's office ostensibly to look for a suicide note. These included Bernard Nussbaum, White House Counsel, Margaret Williams, Chief of Staff to Hillary Clinton, and Deputy Assistant to the President, Patsy Thomasson. When they were later made public, these multiple entries to Foster's office were viewed with great suspicion by some members of the Senate who believed that at least part of the purpose of the visit was to search for and remove incriminating, or at least sensitive, Whitewater and Travelgate documents. The subsequent handling of the documents found in Foster's office and the belated discovery of a suicide note in his briefcase further fuelled the suspicions of critics. Foster's suicide note contains a reference to his concern about the Travelgate scandal.

The Travelgate scandal began in May 1993 when Vincent Foster asked Associate White House Counsel, William Kennedy, yet another former Rose Law Firm partner, to investigate allegations of mismanagement and misappropriation of funds. Seven employees were subsequently sacked and the White House almost immediately came under intense criticism for its handling of the matter. As a result of a White House inquiry and an FBI investigation, William Kennedy was reprimanded and subsequently left the White House. The suggestion was that the allegations of misconduct had been made to ensure the White House travel business was given to friends of Bill and Hillary Clinton. Although Foster was not directly criticized, he seemed to have felt responsible.

The Travelgate storm was still blowing when it was revealed, four months after his death, that there had been documents relating to Whitewater in Foster's office. The delay in disclosure raised further suspicions. When the Justice Department lawyers investigating the Madison Savings and Loan asked for these Whitewater documents, there were delays in producing them and this also fuelled speculation and suspicions. During the same period, the RTC had made further criminal referrals relating to Madison which cited the Clintons as 'potential witnesses'. In October 1993, news of these referrals had leaked and the *Washington Post*, the *Wall Street Journal* and the *New York Times* all ran stories which linked Madison to Whitewater to Bill and Hillary Clinton and to Vincent Foster.

What had once seemed to have been a non-scandal – after all, the Clintons had actually lost money – was now developing rapidly into a real scandal. It was beginning to look as if the Clintons had something to hide, and the suicide of Vince Foster and the Travelgate scandal only made things look worse. By November, the Whitewater scandal was prime-time television news and newscasters reported allegations that Clinton had used his political position as Governor of Arkansas to obtain loans for McDougal, allegations that the Clintons' tax returns were in a mess, and allegations that linked the investigations in Arkansas to Foster's death.

By the end of 1993, political and media pressure was mounting and there were repeated calls for the appointment of an independent counsel.

Strictly speaking, as the Attorney-General, Janet Reno, pointed out, this was not possible because the independent counsel legislation had lapsed in the wake of dissatisfaction about Walsh's seven-year investigation of Iran–Contra. Reno argued that the Justice Department was already investigating Madison and Whitewater, and that for her department to appoint another investigator would lead to duplication and would not give the investigation a more independent status. But political priorities usually triumph over legal niceties and organizational logic and, when influential Democrat Senator Patrick Moynihan (New York) joined the Republican calls for an independent investigation, the pressure became intense. There were divisions in the administration about how to respond and growing concern that Whitewater was derailing President Clinton's legislative agenda. The admission that Whitewater files had been removed from Foster's office caused a media explosion. It was agreed that the files would be turned over to the Justice Department in response to a subpoena but, of course, with the implication they would remain confidential until the Justice Department's investigation was complete. In other words, Congress, the press and the public would not know what the documents contained.

The Chief White House Counsel, Bernard Nussbaum, was vehemently opposed to the appointment of any outside investigator. Ironically, Nussbaum had served as a counsel to the House Judiciary Committee during Watergate and, it seems, he was determined the Clintons would not go through a similar experience. He is reported to have said 'the independent counsel is an evil institution. It is designed to find things out.'[7] More persuasively, Nussbaum argued that it would be wrong to launch an investigation when there was no credible evidence of wrongdoing. A media clamour was not, in his view, a reason for lowering the threshold for appointing an independent counsel. Nussbaum believed, and events proved him correct, that an independent counsel would delve into the affairs of people connected to Clinton and greatly broaden the original area of inquiry. Nussbaum's advice was that, recognizing the political and media pressure, the Clintons should turn over all documents, demand congressional hearings and even offer to testify.

Bill Clinton had grown very irritated that Whitewater would not go away. He found that, even on a visit to Ukraine, the reporters wanted only to talk about Whitewater. Not only would it not go away but Whitewater seemed to be following him everywhere he went. While still in Ukraine, Clinton finally made the decision to appoint a special counsel.

On 20 January 1994, Robert B. Fiske, a moderate Republican, was appointed as special counsel. Fiske had demonstrated political independence by his appointment as a US attorney by President Ford and his reappointment by President Carter in the 1970s. He had alienated more conservative Republicans in the 1980s when, as head of the judicial screening panel of the American Bar Association, he had opposed some Reagan nominees whose qualifications appeared to him to be more ideological than legal.[8] After discussion with Janet Reno, the Attorney-General, the terms of reference for his inquiries were agreed. These terms proved to be elastic and allowed Fiske to roam anywhere he chose.

The appointment of Fiske did little to quell Republican demands for a congressional investigation. The embarrassment caused to President Reagan by congressional Democrats still rankled with Republicans who were keen to ensure that President Clinton suffered a similarly uncomfortable experience. Congressional Democrats tried to counter with the arguments that Whitewater was trivial compared to the Iran–Contra scandal and that any congressional hearings would interfere with the recently appointed special counsel's investigations. They pointed, for example, to the difficulties the Iran–Contra hearings had created for the Iran–Contra independent counsel, Lawrence Walsh, in his efforts to prosecute Oliver North, John Poindexter and others.

Although Whitewater was a 'hot' issue in the White House, in congressional Republican circles and in parts of the media, it had not made much impression on public opinion. The opinion polls in January 1994 suggested that only a minority thought that the Clintons had done anything seriously wrong or illegal, and almost two-thirds thought that congressional hearings were unnecessary.[9] Later opinion-poll evidence suggests that public responses to the scandal were ambiguous depending on the questions posed and that opinions about Whitewater did not have much bearing on Clinton's public-approval ratings. By March 1994, more that half of the respondents said that the Clintons were guilty of something [10] and, by large majorities, both the Senate and the House voted to hold their own investigations while accepting that their hearings should not interfere with the special counsel's investigation.

If the principle of congressional hearings had been accepted, there was still a lot of leeway for partizan political conflict about the scope and limits of the investigations. Given that there were Democrat majorities in both houses of Congress and that it was a Democratic president who was under investigation, it is unsurprising that there was a concerted effort by the majority party to focus narrowly the scope of the inquiry. This could be done partly by using specialist committees such as the Banking Committees and by showing deference to the special counsel's ongoing investigation. Conversely, the Republicans wanted free-ranging, special select committees to roam around looking for damaging information. They complained that, whereas the Watergate and Iran–Contra committees had been given a wide remit, the proposed Whitewater inquiries would be much more restrictive.

The politics of partizan scandal are such that the arguments hardly mattered. There is little doubt that the Democrats' enthusiasm for investigating the activities of the White House had notably cooled now that the incumbent was not a Republican. It can also not be denied that investigations of what a president did many years before he became president are not directly analogous to alleged abuses of presidential power. To Democrats, Whitewater was a pseudo-scandal manufactured by Clinton's enemies, and they were determined not to allow the congressional investigations to become a full-scale 'fishing expedition' permitting unlimited trawling in any direction Clinton's enemies wanted. The Democrats' determination to control the congressional inquiries was illustrated by their choice of the Banking Committees. These committees had large Democrat majorities and this clearly inhibited the ability of the Republican minority to influence the scope and direction of the investigations. Ultimately, if the Republicans wanted Congress to investigate Whitewater, they had to do so on the Democrats' terms.[11]

It was not just the terms of reference that were determined by the Democrats, but also the procedure. When the hearings began, the Democrat Chairman of the House Banking Committee, Henry Gonzales, imposed strict procedural rules which severely inhibited the ability of committee members to interrogate witnesses. In a bizarre move, Gonzales ordered that ten members of the White House staff appear as a panel before the committee and allowed Republican members only a few minutes each to interrogate the entire panel. Through their control of the scope of the investigation and the hearings procedures, the Democrat leadership turned the House investigation into something little short of a farce. Republican hopes of securing greater progress in the Senate Banking Committee were also dashed. Again, strict partizanship was the order of the day, and the restriction on the terms of reference precluded the discovery of even a broken spear, let alone a 'smoking gun'. From the Republican perspective, there was a dual frustration: the public remained indifferent both to Whitewater and to the apparent abuse of congressional investigation procedures. Their task was not helped by a preliminary report by the special counsel, Fiske, which concluded that Foster had committed suicide and which observed that the suicide seemed unrelated either to Whitewater or to Madison Savings and Loan.

At the same time as Fiske was reporting, Congress enacted a new independent counsel law, and Attorney-General, Reno, asked the court of appeal to reappoint Fiske. But Fiske had powerful enemies in the Republican party, and his failure to find anything incriminating in his first report encouraged them to press for a more aggressive independent counsel. Frustrated by what they saw as a mockery of a congressional investigation, an unusual variation of the scandal 'cover-up' theme, whereby the legislative branch seeks to obstruct its own efforts to expose wrongdoing in the executive branch, the new independent counsel seemed in the summer of 1994 to be the Republicans' best hope of capitalizing on Whitewater. In July, the two conservative Republican Senators from North Carolina, Lauch Faircloth and Jesse Helms, lunched with appeal court judge, David B. Sentelle, also from North Carolina, who was a member of the three-judge panel considering the request to reappoint Fiske as independent counsel. All three have denied even discussing Fiske but, in August, it was announced that Fiske was being removed and replaced by Kenneth Starr, a much more conservative Republican who had previously been appointed an appeals court judge by President Reagan and as Solicitor-General by President Bush. The appointment of a man with obvious conservative links brought dismay to the White House which was beginning to think that, with congressional hearings proving a damp squib and the non-incriminating report from Fiske, the worst of Whitewater was behind them.

If the Whitewater scandal was temporarily stalled, the reputations of Bill and Hillary Clinton were being assailed by new side scandals, such as the revelation that Hillary Clinton had speculated in the commodities markets and had received improbably high returns,[12] and Paula Jones's sexual-harassment law suit filed against Bill Clinton. While no further damaging information about Whitewater had emerged, the White House management of it had been flawed, and the Foster suicide, the commodities speculation and the Travelgate scandal had eroded the credibility of key White House staff. The White House was struggling to deal with several scandals at once, and the management of and response to these scandals left much to be desired. Two of President Clinton's key staff, his Chief Counsel, Bernard Nussbaum, and the Treasury Deputy Secretary, Roger Altman, were subsequently forced to resign because of allegations that they had had improper contact on the criminal referrals of Madison Savings and Loan. Numerous White House staff were subject to the indignity of having to face questions from sceptical congressional committees. Overall, the White House was on the defensive; it had taken some casualties but the president's relatively low approval ratings did not seem to be a product of public concern about Whitewater. In November 1994, however, the Clintons' political sky 'fell in' with the Republican capture of Congress for the first time in forty years. This changed the complexion of many issues including the Whitewater scandal.

As is so often the case, the political context defines political scandals and determines their impact. At the beginning of 1995, the political tide for the Clintons was at its lowest ebb. The key health-care reform package had already been defeated in Congress in September 1994. The Republican takeover of Congress implied that the prospects of implementing other parts of the Clinton programme were bleak. Worse still, there would be further congressional inquiries into Whitewater but this time they would be conducted aggressively and according to Republican rules. Clinton's opponents thought that, at last, they had him on the run, and Republicans debated whether to finish him off or whether it was better to keep him in the White House in a weakened state. Some thought that impeachment was a possibility, others believed that Hillary would be indicted and Clinton would be forced to resign. Others favoured the 'haemophiliac approach' – use Whitewater to make Clinton bleed from time to time but make no effort to destroy him for fear of his replacement by his relatively popular and then scandal-free Vice-President, Al Gore.

Yet, by the end of 1995, Clinton's approval ratings had moved above 50 per cent for the first time since 1993. The 'comeback kid' entered the presidential election year of 1996 in much better political shape than it was reasonable to expect a year earlier. This improvement was due to a number of factors. Once in power, the congressional Republicans were more interested in pursuing their own radical agenda than with devoting scarce resources and time to legislative investigations into Whitewater which seemed to be going round in circles. With a conservative independent counsel in place and, moreover, one with a reputation for toughness, it made political sense not to rush into another round of inconclusive hearings but to see what Kenneth Starr's investigations would produce. Conversely, President Clinton, having seen the Democrats repudiated in the polls, was cast almost in the role of leader of the opposition and he attacked the extremism of the new congressional majority and raised public concerns about the future of Medicare and social security.

In April 1995, the Resolution Trust Corporation, which oversaw the failed Savings and Loans, produced its preliminary report on Madison and Whitewater. The head of the investigation was a Republican attorney, Jay Stephens, whose appointment in February 1994 had caused White House aides, notably George Stephanopoulos, to explode with anger. The White House believed that Stephens, a Bush appointee, was angry with the Clinton administration for replacing him as US Attorney for the District of Columbia. Stephens was seen as a political enemy of the Clintons and it is alleged that White House staff tried to get the appointment changed. Stephens's investigation lasted for two years and, while it was going on, the organization that commissioned it had ceased to exist when the activities of the RTC were merged into the Federal Deposit Insurance Corporation.

The Stephens report portrayed the Clintons as passive investors in Whitewater and as uninvolved and unaware of any improper or illegal dealing by Jim McDougal. Although the setting-up of the Stephens inquiry was widely reported, its reports were largely ignored – perhaps a case of good news is no news. Once again hopes of a 'smoking gun' had been raised and then shattered. The lesson of the Stephens report for those who cared to draw it was that the chances of the Arkansas phase of Whitewater yielding any valuable scandal material were becoming remote. In 1995, the focus of scandal clearly shifted away from the precise role of the Clintons in the Whitewater investment and to their alleged secrecy, deception and 'cover-up' of that role once Bill Clinton had reached the White House. One study suggests that 'of 1,070 news stories written about the Whitewater scandal between 1992 and 1996, some 90 per cent have concerned themselves with the cover-up question'.[13]

Congressional hearings on Whitewater did not resume until the summer of 1995, and one consideration in the delay was the desire to continue them into 1996, a presidential election year. Throughout 1995, independent counsel, Kenneth Starr, brought indictments against a number of Arkansas residents, including the Governor of Arkansas, Jim Guy Tucker. The strategy seemed to be to use prosecutions to exercise leverage on the defendants to become more forthcoming with the independent counsel. When the Senate hearings began they focused almost entirely on the conduct of the White House in the period immediately following the death of Vince Foster. The House Banking Committee hearings were much shorter, and focused on the RTC investigation and Arkansas matters. While the chair of the House Banking Committee seemed to have concluded that there was little more to find, the Senate Chair, Alfonse D'Amato (R-NY), was determined to keep his Whitewater hearings going for as long as possible. Senator Faircloth repeatedly demanded that Hillary Clinton should be called to testify but D'Amato argued that it was up to the First Lady to decide whether she wanted to shed any light on what happened following Foster's death. The congressional hearings and the independent counsel's investigation ground on into 1996 and, while there was much speculation, there were few revelations and little in the way of new information.

The Clintons had been subjected to indignities rarely experienced by presidents and first ladies. They were both interviewed on a number of occasions by the independent counsel; Mrs Clinton had to give evidence to a grand jury, and President Clinton gave video-tape evidence in the trials of former Arkansas associates. Similarly, a number of White House officials were required to testify to grand juries and to congressional committees, thereby incurring substantial legal bills. But, by the time the second round of congressional hearings got under way in the summer of 1995, the public was seemingly bored or indifferent to the proceedings. Polls suggested that two thirds thought the hearings were not necessary.[14] The consensus seemed to be that the Clintons were probably not telling the whole truth, that they had probably committed minor offences some years ago and that there were more important issues for politicians to address. A significant minority of 20–30 per cent of respondents remained convinced that the Clintons had done something seriously wrong even if it had not yet been possible to prove it.

The D'Amato Senate Committee finally reported in the summer of 1996.[15] Unsurprisingly, the committee divided on partizan lines and there was a minority Democrat report that dissented sharply from the conclusions and analysis of the majority Republican report. The majority report was highly critical but stopped short of making criminal allegations. It suggested that, by the time of Foster's death, the Clintons had established a pattern of concealing their involvement with Whitewater and the McDougals' Madison Savings and Loan. It argues that Foster's office contained damaging evidence about the Whitewater and Travelgate scandals, and alleges that a number of White House officials and Mrs Clinton herself were engaged in improper conduct in the removal and handling of documents from Foster's office. It asserts that many White House staff gave incomplete and inaccurate testimony to the special committee and insists that the Office of the White House Counsel was misused to impede ongoing investigations.

The Senate Committee found that senior White House officials improperly gathered confidential information about investigations involving Whitewater and Madison Savings and Loan and that they sought to manipulate investigations into this improper conduct. It accused White House officials of confusing the personal legal interests of President and Mrs Clinton with their official roles. As far as the files of the Rose Law Firm are concerned, their disappearance and reappearance are depicted as part of a pattern of removal, concealment and, at times, destruction of records concerning Mrs Clinton's legal work on behalf of Madison Savings and Loan. The Senate Committee comes close but does not actually accuse Mrs Clinton personally of concealing documents. The phrase chosen is 'Mrs Clinton is more likely than any other known individual'.[16]

With regard to the original scandal, the Whitewater investment and the Clintons' involvement with the McDougals, the committee concludes that the conviction of the McDougals and other associates of the Clintons confirmed that the Whitewater scandal could no longer be seen as a 'cover-up without a crime'. In the committee's view, the Arkansas jury unanimously concluded that Jim McDougal operated Madison Savings and Loan as, in effect, a criminal enterprise. According to the committee, it is now clear that Madison Savings and Loan and other investment companies were 'piggy banks for the Arkansas political elite'.[17] It suggests that the Clintons were active in obtaining and extending Whitewater-related loans and that they were not the 'passive' investors they have always claimed to be. It concludes that the Clintons made a series of erroneous tax deductions relating to Whitewater and that Governor Clinton's official and personal dealings with Jim McDougal raised an apparent, if not actual, improper conflict of interest.

The majority report alleges misconduct, obstruction of investigations and appearance of wrongdoing but it makes no specific allegations against the Clintons or White House officials that could be subject to legal test. The minority report, conversely, seeks to deny any wrongdoing and refutes the allegations in the majority report. With regard to the Foster inquiry, the minority concludes that the conduct of the White House staff on the night in question was motivated by good intentions and influenced by shock and grief. In relation to the Rose Law Firm billing records, the minority report dismisses the majority's concern at the disappearance and reappearance of the records and concentrates on the extent to which the records actually support Mrs Clinton's previous testimony about the work she performed for Madison Savings and Loan. It found no interference in the investigations of Madison Savings and Loan but rather a congressional investigation shaped by political motives. It concluded that the criminal referral was handled properly and there were no improper meetings or disclosures of confidential information. It found that the Clintons corrected past errors in their personal tax returns, errors committed only because of a lack of information about the Whitewater investment. Contrary to the majority report, it found that the Clintons were, as they claimed, passive investors in Whitewater. It points out that the RTC reports on Madison Savings and Loan made no finding of illegal or improper activity by the Clintons. It finds that false accusations had been made against Bill Clinton by individuals seeking plea-bargains and immunity for testimony.

In short, the Senate Special Committee on Whitewater produced two contradictory and incompatible reports on Whitewater. A year-long investigation produced a few nuggets of new information but nothing conclusive. To some this was evidence of incomplete and evasive testimony, the destruction of records and worse, while, to others, this confirmed that, all along, Whitewater was a politically motivated investigation 'in search of a scandal'.

Since the reports of the Whitewater Special Committee, the focus of the Whitewater scandal has shifted from Congress to the prosecution of the Clintons' business partners and friends, Jim and Susan McDougal and the long-awaited report of the independent counsel, Kenneth Starr. The year 1996 was a presidential election year and Democrats did not miss the connections between those investigating the Clintons and political interests hostile to his re-election. Not only was Senator Alfonse D'Amato the Chairman of the Senate Special Committee, but he was also the co-chairman of Bob Dole's presidential campaign. Independent counsel, Kenneth Starr, was defined as a Republican activist who continued to represent tobacco companies in conflict with the White House.

In the meantime, one of the original partners in Whitewater, Susan McDougal, was sentenced in August 1996, to two years' imprisonment for fraud. In September, the independent counsel subpoenaed her to testify before the Whitewater grand jury. She was asked directly whether she had discussed an illegal loan with Bill Clinton and whether President Clinton had perjured himself in his trial testimony. She declined to answer and was sent to prison for contempt. Susan McDougal claims that the independent counsel offered leniency in exchange for evidence incriminating the Clintons. In her view, Starr and his team are interested only in destroying the Clintons. Her ex-husband Jim McDougal's sentence was deferred for a year after his multiple convictions for fraud to encourage co-operation with the independent counsel. Susan McDougal alleged that her husband was lying to Starr in the hope of leniency. Jim McDougal was eventually sentenced, in April 1997, to three years' imprisonment after Starr's recommendation that he receive a reduced sentence.

In February 1997, the independent counsel, Kenneth Starr, announced he was giving up his post in August to take up a position at Pepperdine University in California. Pepperdine University has received substantial donations from right-wing foundations hostile to the Clintons. A few days later, Starr announced that he had made an error of judgement and that he would be staying on to complete his investigations. To date, his investigations have proved relatively free of leaks but reports suggest that he has concluded that Foster did commit suicide and that the Clintons were not involved in a cover-up.[18] Until Starr submits his report, it will not be possible to draw a line under the Whitewater scandal. If Starr recommends the prosecution of White House staff, Mrs Clinton or even President Clinton himself, the trials will take months and even years to exhaust the legal process. In the unlikely event that President Clinton is charged, the trial would not take place until after he leaves office. In this case, a failed land speculation in the 1970s will have smouldered as a political scandal into the twenty-first century.

The Whitewater scandal seems to have taken on a life of its own. It is still regularly reported but its impact on Clinton's approval ratings has long been discounted, and clearly it did not impede his re-election in November 1996. It surfaced only briefly and belatedly in the Republican presidential campaign in relation to the possible granting of pardons by Clinton to the McDougals or members of his staff. The issue never developed real momentum and was partly defused by reminders from the Iran–Contra independent counsel, Lawrence Walsh, that Bob Dole had previously urged pardons for Reagan's senior staff caught up in Walsh's investigations.

Given the absence to date of incriminating evidence and legal charges against the Clintons and their senior staff, the longevity of the Whitewater scandal is unusual. There seems almost to be a 'Whitewater industry' which, rather like that surrounding the assassination of President Kennedy, generates a lot of publicity. To understand the persistence of the Whitewater scandal, it is necessary to examine how and why it has been sustained.

Media Accounts of Whitewater

There is little doubt that much of the reporting of Whitewater emanates from sources that are personally and politically hostile to the Clintons. In particular, conspiracy theories have enjoyed wide publicity and, through being reported in the mainstream media, have achieved greater credence than they otherwise would. One man's conspiracy may be another's paranoia and one man's fearless quest after truth may be another's obsession but, by 1995, the White House was so concerned at the reporting of Whitewater that it developed its own explanation of how the scandal was sustained by the media.[19]

The White House sees a collection of well-funded right-wing think tanks and individuals as the beginning of the 'media food chain'. These include the Western Journalism Centre (WJC) and the Landmark Legal Foundation (LLF), Accuracy in Media (AIM) and Citizens United. The WJC is funded largely by foundations controlled by Richard Mellon Scaife who is close to Newt Gingrich. The WJC sponsored full-page advertisements in the *New York Times* and the *Washington Post* asking whether Foster's death was a suicide. The advertisements were actually reprints of an article published in the *Pittsburgh Tribune – Review* which is also published by Scaife. The LLF receives funding from a variety of conservative groups including the Scaife foundation. The LLF has filed ethics complaints against Congressman David Bonior who had lodged complaints against Gingrich and has represented L. Jean Lewis, the RTC investigator in Whitewater, and former Attorney-General, Edwin Meese, in the Iran–Contra scandal. Citizens United was founded in 1988 by Floyd Brown as a conservative reaction to the opponents of Supreme Court nominee, Robert Bork.

These organizations produce a regular supply of articles, newsletters, videos, advertisements and television programmes designed to permeate the mainstream media. They also make extensive use of the internet and, in some ways, Whitewater can be seen as the first internet scandal which allows Whitewater conspiracy theorists to disseminate their allegations and interpretations. The second stage of the 'media food chain' is for these stories and theories to be picked up by the conservative press both in the United States and in Britain, in particular the *Wall Street Journal*, the *Washington Times* and the *Sunday Telegraph*. The White House suggests there is 'transatlantic blowback' whereby right-wing conspiracy theories are published in British newspapers and then taken up by American newspapers citing the British newspapers as their authority. In such situations, there is less need for corroboration, wild stories are recycled and, in consequence, 'some of the British coverage of Clinton has been "certifiably insane"'.[20]

Once the conspiracy theories appear in respectable conservative newspapers, it sets off demands for further official inquiries both by Congress and by independent counsels. When such demands are made, the demands and the stories which gave rise to them are faithfully reported in the mainstream media. Once official inquiries begin, they too are also regularly reported in the mainstream media. The point here is that there is always more than one scandal and each scandal is multi-faceted, and so there is a cycle of scandalmongering, a continuous supply for the 'media food chain'.

It is not necessary to accept completely the White House's theory of scandal communication to recognize that the Clintons have a large number of well-funded enemies. The depth of enmity the Clintons engender can be illustrated by the remarks of retired Arkansas Supreme Court Justice, Jim Johnson, who apologized to a Conservative Political Action conference in 1993 for Arkansas having given the nation a president who is a 'queer-mongering, whore-hopping adulterer; a baby-killing, draft-dodging, dope-tolerating, lying, two-faced, treasonous activist'.[21] Johnson assisted the Director of Citizens United, David Bossie, to gather 'dirt' on the Clintons. Bossie maintained active contact with networks of reporters, television producers and congressional aides as he sought to generate and sustain interest in the Whitewater and 'Troopergate' scandals. While conservative interest groups mobilized against Clinton, conservative journalists like David Brock practised a new form of openly ideological journalism in magazines like the

American Spectator, a magazine funded by Richard Scaife and whose stories were taken up by a number of conservative talk-show hosts, notably Rush Limbaugh. Bossie accumulated his own library on White-water and, to save journalists time, he supplied them with volumes he had compiled on different aspects of Whitewater. He moved on to providing information to the House committee investigating Whitewater and also briefed Senators D'Amato and Faircloth. Citizens United is credited with originating stories in *Money*, *US News and World Report*, the *Wall Street Journal* and on NBC television. Eventually, Bossie re-signed from Citizens United during the summer of 1995 to join the staff of Senator Faircloth, a member of the Senate committee investigating Whitewater. When Arkansas Senator, David Pryor, described Citizens United as 'a poison factory', Bossie replied with 2,500 faxes to media outlets suggesting that Pryor had improperly intervened to secure a job for one of Clinton's staff. As Stewart observes, 'the counter attack served not only as retaliation for Pryor, but as a warning to any legislator who might be thinking of coming to the Clintons' defense'.[22]

But to accept that there has been a wealth of deeply hostile coverage of Whitewater does not mean that such attacks are entirely fabricated or represent some orchestrated conspiracy. Conspiracy theorists are unwilling to accept mistakes and coincidences, and they refuse to believe that officials ever operate from admirable motives but, nonetheless, there are sometimes conspiracies. The efforts of the right-wing press and interest groups to discredit Clinton were sustained not merely by private wealth but by the way the Clintons and their staff have re-sponded to the emerging Whitewater scandal. The conclusion to this chapter will consider Whitewater in its political and media contexts and what they reveal about the management and style of the Clinton Presidency.

Conclusion

While some of the wilder internet accounts of Whitewater depict Vince Foster as an agent of the Israeli secret service, it is reasonably safe to assume that the Whitewater scandal raises no serious issues of national security. Whitewater is not a scandal about a criminal conspiracy to obstruct justice, an undeclared war, an illegal sale of arms, a circumven-tion of a congressional resolution, unlawful surveillance, government-sponsored burglary, government-financed terrorism or any other high crimes or misdemeanours. To this extent, it is profoundly different from

Watergate and Iran–Contra. Yet, despite these differences, Whitewater resembles earlier presidential scandals in a number of respects.

The origins of Whitewater as a scandal are relatively easy to date. There is the proto-scandal of the first *New York Times* article in March 1992, which makes the crucial links between the McDougals and Clintons and between Whitewater and Madison Savings and Loan. As was described earlier, this had been relatively well handled by the then presidential candidate, Clinton, who ensured that an ostensibly independent investigation 'proved' that the Clintons had lost money on their Whitewater investment. The turning point in the scandal was the death of Vince Foster in May 1993. The sudden and apparently inexplicable death of a senior public official known to be close to the president and his wife was bound to cause a firestorm of media and public interest. Suspicion and speculation were rife and the handling of the police investigation seemed unsatisfactory. Reports that Foster had been murdered fuelled even wilder rumours and speculations. It was therefore almost inevitable that Foster's personal and professional relationship with the Clintons, and the conduct of Mrs Clinton and the White House staff in the immediate aftermath of Foster's death, would be subject to close scrutiny. When it belatedly emerged that Foster's office had contained papers relevant to the recently broken Travelgate scandal as well as to Whitewater, the full scandal now known as Whitewater came into being. Like Frankenstein's monster, its origins then seemed unimportant and it developed in ways that could not be foreseen.

It is important to note that, in political terms, Whitewater is effectively a multiple scandal, an umbrella term given to describe both different periods and aspects of Whitewater but which also includes the later scandals of Travelgate and Filegate which have been assigned for investigation to the Whitewater independent counsel, Kenneth Starr. Indeed, part of Starr's explanation for the delay in his report on Whitewater is that these other matters were referred to him more recently and require thorough investigation. Starr's report could be the decisive final act in the Whitewater drama. If he finds no serious wrongdoing on the part of the Clintons or any of their current staff, Whitewater will probably be classified as the largest, most expensive and most partisan non-scandal in American political history. Conversely, if the First Lady, Hillary Clinton, is accused of illegal conduct and prosecution seems likely, the political consequences are incalculable but could involve the end of the Clinton Presidency. In March 1997, the gossip inside the Washington 'beltway' was that some White House staff, past and present, would face charges; that Hillary Clinton would be heavily criticized but not charged; and that President Clinton would escape relatively unscathed. If this scenario is right, the Clinton Presidency would be safe and perhaps Whitewater will occupy a special place as the first First Lady scandal rather than be seen as a major presidential scandal.

One of the interesting issues raised in the Whitewater scandal is the appointment and the role of the White House staff. There is a well-established practice of key White House posts being assigned to prominent members of the presidential campaign team. There is another and closely related practice of giving important posts to people who originate from the same state as the president. There are obvious and good reasons for these practices: the people are demonstrably loyal to the president; they have been tried and tested; and the president knows and trusts them. But there are also dangers in assuming that those who are skilled in the arts of campaigning are also skilled in the arts of governing and managing. When localism is a factor in appointment, there are special problems if the president comes from a particularly small state like Arkansas, where the pool of talent is markedly shallower than in California or New York. The Arkansas political circle is very small and it was almost certain that an ambitious politician like Bill Clinton would know all of the political players and meet them in a variety of contexts.

Bill Clinton first met Jim McDougal when they both worked for the legendary Arkansas politician, Senator J. William Fulbright. McDougal subsequently helped Fulbright make money in a land deal. When Clinton became Governor of Arkansas, he briefly employed McDougal as an adviser on economic development. McDougal left to go into land speculation and, just as he had made money for one Arkansas luminary, Fulbright, so Whitewater was a way of making money for another of his political friends, Bill Clinton. Governors of small states are not well paid, and the prospect of obtaining a substantial sum was obviously tempting to the Clintons. At the same time, Hillary Clinton's partnership in the Rose Law Firm probably owes much to her husband's political profile in Arkansas. When Bill Clinton was elected President of the United States, no fewer than four partners in the Rose Law Firm (Hillary Clinton, Webster Hubbell, Vincent Foster, William Kennedy) went to Washington with him. Only Hillary Clinton is still with him.

Hillary Clinton is believed to have had a major impact on the appointment of key cabinet members, and presumably must share some of the responsibility for 'nannygate', the difficulty in finding a female attorney-general who hired only legal immigrants and paid social security taxes. Mrs Clinton also had responsibility for co-ordinating health care reform proposals. Not only was she severely criticized and legally challenged for the way the proposal was assembled but, of course, it was defeated in Congress. Since 1993, Mrs Clinton has adopted a more traditional First Lady role and has not been seen as a powerful force in policy-making. Uniquely, Mrs Clinton's approval ratings have tended to be lower than her husband's.

Webster Hubbell was appointed Associate Attorney General and was Clinton's point man in the Justice Department, Clinton's own 'Hubbell telescope'. Absent the search for diversity, and Hubbell may have been a candidate for Attorney-General. Hubbell was brought down indirectly by Whitewater through the investigations of the Rose Law Firm. When the investigations of Madison Savings and Loan moved from the RTC to the Justice Department, Hubbell had to recuse (remove) himself from overseeing the investigation because of his association with the Clintons. But the inquiries into the Rose Law Firm and its relation to the Savings and Loan were conducted partly through an examination of the billing records. These revealed that Hubbell had been overcharging clients in a substantial way. This led to Hubbell's resignation and his subsequent prosecution and imprisonment.[23] The third partner, William Kennedy, was severely criticized for his role in the 'Travelgate' scandal and was another victim of 'nannygate'. He subsequently resigned from his position as Associate Counsel to the President. The fourth partner in the Rose Law Firm and the tragic figure of the Whitewater scandal was Vince Foster, Deputy Counsel to the President, who, according to the police, a coroner and two independent counsels, committed suicide in May 1993. Of four members of the same law firm and members of Little Rock's social elite, one is sidelined and would have resigned or been fired if she had been allowed to have a government job; one resigned and went back to Little Rock; one went to prison; and one killed himself.

Some explanations of Whitewater interpret it in terms of a problem of cultural adaptation, a failure to understand that Washington was not Little Rock and that patterns of behaviour and styles of government established in a small southern state were not appropriate or acceptable at the centre of the national government. If Little Rock is a town where everyone knows everyone else, Washington is run periodically by a 'government of strangers' new to federal politics and often new to one another. This creates problems in ensuring effective communication and co-ordination both in the White House and between the White House and other government entities. Layered on top of the problem of parochial figures playing national roles is the unprecedented role of the First Lady and the management style of President Clinton himself. Hillary Clinton held no post in the White House, but White House staff and those who had dealings with the White House knew she was a powerful player in the inner circle of decision-makers. President Clinton's management style has attracted various descriptions, but 'disciplined', 'consistent' and 'structured' are not often among the terms used. This combination of 'Arkansas come to Washington', a powerful First Lady and a president whose enthusiasms and interests normally override concerns for order and clarity encouraged particular sorts of response to Whitewater and its associated scandals.

Bill Clinton came to the White House promising the most ethical administration ever and, in the middle of a spate of independent counsel investigations of members of his administration, he asserted 'Everyone knows that I have tougher ethics rules than any previous President'.[24] It is certainly the case that post-employment restrictions on government officials have been tightened up but it is not clear that there has been corresponding attention directed to what the officials do during their government service. One recent study concludes that the Clinton Administration has caused a further erosion of public confidence in the integrity of the federal government. In particular, it alleges that 'the White House has conducted itself often as if it were oblivious to ethical concerns', its responses have served to exacerbate the public's suspicion of wrongdoing and, above all, 'the President and White House have displayed a fundamental lack of candor'.[25]

The accounts given by the Clintons of their involvement in Whitewater, about Mrs Clinton's commodity speculations, about their tax returns, about Mrs Clinton's Rose Law Firm billing records, and about Mrs Clinton's involvement in Travelgate have not always been characterized by complete openness or a compulsion to disclose. Documents and records have initially been withheld and divulged only in response to political or media pressure or ultimately in answer to a subpoena. Too often, these delays have been depicted as obstruction or even 'cover-up' and this has had important consequences. It seems that, having agreed a line of defence, the Clintons are reluctant to leave it even when their conduct is not in question. Having described themselves as passive investors in Whitewater, there seemed to be a reluctance to acknowledge that Mrs Clinton had assumed power of attorney over the Whitewater Development Corporation. But the collapse of Madison Savings and Loan and Jim McDougal's physical and mental ill health meant that there was no one to deal with the Whitewater debt deadlines except Mrs Clinton. It seems that she reacted properly to the need to deal with their creditors but was reluctant to admit to an active role in Whitewater.

The impression given by the conduct of the Clintons in response to inquiries about their financial affairs in the 1970s is one of resistance. They have sought to protect their privacy and, when this has involved their financial records, the appearance has been created that they have something to hide. The tendency and inclination of the White House to stonewall in the face of questions and criticism gave the media a licence to be irresponsible. They could report rumours about Whitewater and, in the absence of specific White House refutation, the media bore no responsibility for the veracity or accuracy of their allegations. The Clinton White House's approach to allegations and charges has been characterized as 'a circle the wagons attitude, categorical denials made by persons without personal knowledge of the facts, the withholding of relevant documents and impugning the motives of those raising ethics concerns'.[26]

The Clintons' defensive response to Whitewater is understandable in terms of a desire to protect personal privacy, a belief that the allegations are politically inspired, a determination to avoid being diverted from their substantive policy agenda, and a sense of their own righteousness. But such defensiveness gives an appearance of obfuscation and obstruction to the media and wider public. A leading columnist observed in 1994 that 'If the Clintons have nothing to hide, why do they seem to be hiding things? ... the Clintons' problem lies not with Whitewater but in a White House permeated by a hatred of the press, a resentment of disclosure and an attitude of permanent embattlement'.[27] This is an exaggerated conclusion but it focuses on the core of the Clintons' problem in dealing with Whitewater. Elements of the mainstream press, notably the conservative *Washington Times* and the *Wall Street Journal*, have kept Whitewater on the front page, and the *Wall Street Journal*'s attacks on Vince Foster before his suicide caused deep resentment in the White House. The Clintons seemed to have believed both that they could defend a zone of personal privacy, and that when the source of a scandalous allegation is politically tainted, the substance of the allegations does not need to be answered.

The Whitewater scandal has effectively run its course. Its shape and development have clearly been influenced by previous presidential scandals and by the increasing partisan use of scandal as a political weapon. Compared to Watergate, Whitewater has thus far failed to yield a water-pistol let alone a 'smoking gun'. It has not driven Clinton from office nor prevented his re-election. It has been sustained by a combination of partisan attacks, a lack of candour in the White House and the institutional mechanisms of the independent counsel created in the aftermath of Watergate.

It began as an isolated news story in a major newspaper which used an unsuccessful land speculation to link a presidential candidate to a failed Savings and Loan. The widespread bankruptcies in the Savings and Loan industry created a financial scandal unprecedented in American history. Many politicians at both federal and state levels shared the responsibility for the policy and regulatory disaster, and few were bold enough to point the finger of blame. The scale of the Savings and Loan collapse made it relatively easy for the Clinton campaign team to engage in effective scandal management. The Clintons had no direct links to Madison Savings and Loan, and their land speculation seemed to have lost them money. At a time when other Savings and Loans were costing taxpayers billions of dollars, the Clinton story was comparatively trivial and parochial.

But however adroit the Clinton scandal-managers were, the double blow of Travelgate and, more particularly, the dramatic and tragic suicide of Vince Foster moved the Whitewater scandal up to a different level of media coverage and public interest. The White House made a number of mistakes and errors of judgement in its handling of these events, and the familiar scandal machinery of independent investigation and congressional hearings could not be denied. The partisan wrangling about Cox's role in Watergate and Walsh's Ahab-like search for the whale of Iran–Contra had left the legislative framework for investigation in temporary disarray, but political and media pressures forced the attorney-general to appoint a special counsel who effectively enjoyed the discretion and freedom of an authentic independent counsel. Once this appointment was made and, more particularly, when Fiske was replaced by Starr as independent counsel, the White House lost control of Whitewater. As Clinton's former counsel, Bernard Nussbaum, warned, the independent counsel statute is a licence to roam freely anywhere the investigator feels like going. There is no executive-branch control and no effective means of making an independent counsel accountable for his actions.

The ties of party were strong enough to ensure that the Democrat chairs of the Senate and House Banking Committees, Don Riegle and Henry Gonzalez, conducted phoney hearings into Whitewater. This not only infuriated the Republicans in Congress who accused the Democrats of double standards and hypocrisy but it ensured that, when the Republicans gained control of Congress in 1994, there would be a fresh round of congressional hearings with terms of reference and procedural rules that suited the Republican majority. Given the momentum generated by the independent counsel's inquiries and the two sets of congressional hearings, the White House's scope for damage control was limited.

What looks like the final chapter in Whitewater is the report of the independent counsel and associated prosecutions. As expected, once the rock over Little Rock had been lifted, sundry members of the Arkansas business and political elite have been caught engaging in illegal financial dealings. Jim and Susan McDougal, the Clintons' partners in Whitewater, are now in prison. Jim McDougal's co-operation with the independent counsel seems to have been motivated by his disappointment that President Clinton had not pardoned his ex-wife, Susan McDougal. The tactic of the independent counsel is to apply maximum leverage in the plea-bargaining process to ensure that anyone with hard evidence against Bill and Hillary Clinton is 'encouraged' to divulge it. A criminal trial of a First Lady would be a first in American history. The prospect of a president serving out his term before facing criminal prosecutions is almost unthinkable. If, on the other hand, the Clintons are criticized but not prosecuted, there will be many who ask whether four years of investigation and the expenditure of many millions of dollars were justified. Whitewater demonstrates that the appetite for presidential scandal is undiminished, and it further demonstrates that, once the motors of scandal have been started, they can prove costly and difficult to stop.

Notes

1. The literature on Whitewater is unsatisfactory. Many accounts are speculative and overtly hostile to the Clintons. The least unsatisfactory is James B. Stewart, *Blood Sport: The President and His Adversaries* (New York: Simon and Schuster, 1996). But Stewart's grasp of the detail is not always certain and he seems to rely excessively on the veracity of Jim McDougal.
2. *New York Times*, 8 March 1992.

3. Ibid.

4. Stewart, p. 228.

5. Stewart, p. 226.

6. Ellen Joan Pollock, 'Vince Foster's Death is a Lively Business for Conspiracy Buffs', *Wall Street Journal*, 23 March 1995.

7. Stewart, p. 370.

8. Fiske had been nominated as Deputy Attorney-General in 1989 but withdrew when fourteen conservative Senators wrote to President Bush opposing his appointment. See 'Too Much Baggage', *Wall Street Journal*, 21 January 1994.

9. *Newsweek* poll reported a 19 per cent positive response to the question, Are the Clintons guilty of serious offences? (January 1994); *NBC/Wall Street Journal* reported that 61 per cent thought congressional hearings were not necessary (January 1994).

10. *Times Mirror* poll found that 52 per cent believed they were guilty of minor offences, 15 per cent believed they had committed major offences and only 13 per cent thought they were entirely innocent (March 1994).

11. For an analysis of the first round of congressional hearings, see Peter Falconer, 'Whitewater, Partisanship and U.S. Congressional Oversight', *Talking Politics*, September 1995, pp. 53–8.

12. This story was broken by Jeff Gerth who published the first Whitewater story two years earlier: see Jeff Gerth, with Dean Bacquet and Stephen Labaton, 'Top Arkansas Lawyer Helped Hillary Clinton Turn Big Profit', *New York Times*, 18 March 1994.

13. Alexander Cockburn and Ken Silverstein, *Washington Babylon* (London and New York: Verso, 1996), p. 251.

14. *NBC/Wall Street Journal* poll found 63 per cent believed the hearings were not necessary (August 1995).

15. US Senate, *The Special Committee's Whitewater Report* (Washington: Government Printing Office, 1996).

16. *Special Committee; Whitewater Report*, p. 301.

17. Ibid, p. 560.

18. *Los Angeles Times*, 23 February 1997.

19. John F. Harris and Peter Baker, 'White House Asserts a Scandal Theory, *Washington Post*, 10 January 1997, p. A01.

20. Martin Walker, Washington Bureau Chief for *The Guardian*, as reported in the *Washington Post*, 3 May 1994.

21. Quoted in Stewart, p. 314.

22. Stewart, p. 381.

23. Allegations have recently been made that Hubbell was engaged in dubious lobbying and fund-raising activities before the 1996 presidential election. See Michael Duffy, 'Hubbell's Growing Web', *Time Magazine*, 17 February 1997.

24. *Weekly Compilation of Presidential Documents*, 353, 3 March 1995.

25. Gregory S. Walden, *On Best Behaviour: The Clinton Administration and Ethics in Government* (Indianapolis: Hudson Institute, 1996), p. 5.

26. Waldon, p. 13.

27. E. J. Dionne, 'Whitewater: Who Made This Monster?', *Washington Post*, 22 March 1994, p. A17.

CHAPTER 5

Political Scandals in Congress

This chapter is rather different in form from the chapters dealing with the major presidential scandals of the past twenty-five years. Congressional scandals differ in their origins, character and consequence. The president, any president, is the centre of national political and media attention and, as such, his behaviour and misbehaviour attract an enormous amount of attention. While the routine business of the president regularly attracts a great deal of national and international attention, the president's involvement in apparently scandalous conduct provokes the equivalent of a nuclear explosion from the mass media.

Congress is a body of 535 individuals rather than a single person and, other things being equal, it is obvious that public knowledge and awareness of the activities of individual legislators are bound to be relatively low. But things are not equal, and there is no equivalence in terms of the president's capacity to take decisions, to make news, available to an individual senator or representative. Individual legislators influence rather than determine events, and the scandals they attract tend to focus on personal corruption rather than on illegal actions or policy decisions. No legislator is individually responsible for determining the course of the government, passing or vetoing a law, appointing or refusing to confirm a senior official or launching a covert action programme. As legislators' range of scandalous conduct is thereby restricted, scandals involving them tend to focus on their relationships with their staff and with their constituents in general and relationships with their campaign contributors in particular.

If scandal involves behaviour which is improper, illegal or otherwise unacceptable, it follows that legislators need to understand what constitutes proper conduct and where the boundaries of unacceptable conduct lie. These have proved difficult to define both because they have rarely been made explicit and because they have evolved over time, often in response to scandals. Thus, scandals sometimes arise because legislators are behaving in accordance with a code or practice which has become outmoded. The judgement made on allegations of corrupt behaviour is contemporary not historical and, in consequence, legislators experience criticism, censure, expulsion and even imprisonment when they fail to adapt their behaviour to changing expectations about stand-ards of official conduct.

A second difference concerns the way in which legislators are re-garded by the electorate. Viewed collectively, members of Congress are not people who inspire public trust and thus, when allegations of scandal are made, they are likely to be widely believed. There is a strongly held perception that members of Congress are not interested in the concerns of ordinary people but rather are out to line their own pockets by serving special interests. A Gallup Poll in 1992 invited respondents to rank the professional ethics of a variety of occupational groups, and it found that members of Congress were placed substantially below professional groups such as doctors, lawyers and professors. It is true that they were ranked slightly above car salesmen but they were still below estate agents.

Presidents come and go but it seems that legislators go on forever. A new president is a sort of Halley's Comet racing across the political sky. He adds light, colour and excitement but, after he disappears, the political scene returns to its normal ways of working. While a new president can generate hope, belief and even optimism among the elect-orate, Congress seems to be always the same, and the public fears the worst. While a new president is said to enjoy a 'honeymoon' period, Congress projects an enduring image of stalemate and conflict. If the presidency has been periodically rocked by major scandals, Congress seems to be almost permanently afflicted by scandal allegations. Al-though none of these congressional scandals has attracted the length, breadth and intensity of media coverage of Watergate, Iran–Contra or Whitewater, they nonetheless serve to sustain and to reinforce the public image of Congress as a scandal-ridden institution.

Scandals such as Koreagate and Abscam suggest to some that mem-bers of Congress are available for hire by anyone who can afford their prices, including non-US citizens and agents of foreign governments. Scandals involving apparently direct exchanges of campaign money for influence over the operation of federal agencies, such as the Keating Five scandal, suggest that members of Congress perform services for some constituents they do not perform for others. Scandals involving leaders in Congress, such as the Dan Rostenkowski scandal, suggest that leaders in Congress use their official positions to derive personal financial and material benefits. The scandals involving Speakers Jim Wright and Newt Gingrich suggest that high-profile figures in Congress seek to exploit every apparent loophole in campaign and taxation regulations for their personal and political benefit. The House Banking scandal suggests that, collectively, members of Congress are determined to enjoy financial benefits and opportunities not available to members of the public.

For much of the history of Congress, there has been institutional indifference to scandals involving members of the House and Senate. Until relatively recently, scandalous allegations about the behaviour of members have not been investigated by Congress itself but left to the judgement of the member's electorate. This attitude was presumably derived from a desire to avoid sitting in judgement on colleagues and from the belief that, if the member was re-elected, the scandal and the allegations were either unproven or unimportant. But, since the 1960s, there has been a growing awareness of, and sensitivity toward, the decline in levels of public trust and confidence in Congress and an increased institutional commitment to responding to scandalous allegations of impropriety and misbehaviour by senators and representatives. The evident desire and determination of Congress to investigate any and every whisper of scandal in the executive branch have reinforced the political need to demonstrate that Congress takes seriously scandal allegations against members of the House and the Senate.

The Senate established its first ethics committee, the Select Committee on Standards and Conduct in 1964. It was organized on a bipartizan basis but activated only in 1965 after the resolution of the long-running Bobby Baker scandal had been concluded on terms acceptable to the Democratic majority. Following the high-profile scandals involving Representative Adam Clayton Powell, the House of Representatives established its first ethics committee in 1967. But the political fallout from the Baker and Powell cases, together with the scandals associated with Senator Thomas Dodd,[1] prompted both the House and the Senate to adopt their first formal codes of conduct in 1968. The Watergate scandal had ripple effects in Congress and, in 1977, both chambers adopted even more stringent codes of conduct as a condition of a salary increase. These codes of conduct imposed restrictions that legislators had regarded as unthinkable ten years earlier. They limited the outside earned income of members, abolished office accounts and required full disclosure of income, financial holdings, debts, securities and gifts. If, in the 1960s, there was only a hazy understanding of what constituted improper and scandalous conduct, by the 1990s, the House Committee on Standards of Official Conduct was publishing an ethics manual which ran to over 300 pages.[2] In 1978, the Ethics in Government Act was passed which applied to all public officials, legislative as well as executive.

But the institutional efforts of Congress, considerable as they have been, have achieved little in preventing scandals or in improving public confidence in legislators. Scandals now seem an almost integral part of congressional life. Rather than choose one scandal to exemplify all aspects of political scandals in Congress, this chapter will discuss a number of scandals to explain their origins, dynamics, diversity and consequences.

Congressional scandals can be collective as well as singular, and it is important to consider examples where a group of legislators has been the subject of scandal allegations. These may be cases where there has been an attempt to combine for a common purpose, such as maximizing the pressure on particular officials, or cases where a number of individual legislators have independently chosen to behave in the same allegedly improper way, such as by accepting money from the same source. The examples chosen for discussion here are the lobbying activities of a South Korean national, Tongsun Park, or what is popularly known at 'Korea-gate', 1977–8;[3] Abscam,[4] the FBI 'sting' operation designed to trap public officials suspected of corruption in 1980–2; the Keating Five scandal,[5] involving five Senators and their interventions on behalf of the owner of a savings and loan business in 1989–91; and the House Banking scandal,[6] involving the use of overdraft facilities in 1991–2. These scandals, though in one sense collective, were provoked by very different kinds of behaviour, and attracted a wide range of different consequences for the members of Congress concerned. The links between individual culpability, group guilt and the severity or otherwise of the consequences will be discussed later but, for the present, it is sufficient to note that such links are not self-evident and seem to depend more on the political culture and context than on the scandalous behaviour itself.

But members of the United States Congress are notoriously and distinctively individual in their approaches to political life. Unlike their British counterparts, they are largely free from the yoke of party discipline and, of course, the separation of the executive branch from the legislative means that the administration is unable to direct their conduct.

Members of Congress are largely responsible for funding and organizing their election campaigns and, while this poses a variety of problems, it gives a degree of independence from institutional and party leaders which is unprecedented in any other Western democracy. In this sense, members of Congress are free agents who come together with different colleagues for specific purposes but they are not rigidly bound by institutional or party ties.

The task of exercising leadership in an organization composed of independently funded and independently minded individuals is especially taxing, particularly as the leaders largely lack the resources to induce or to coerce their colleagues to behave in ways contrary to the member's perception of his or her own self-interest. In the past twenty-five years, the decentralizing tendencies inherent in Congress have been accelerated by the committee and subcommittee reforms as well as by the erosion of the seniority rule. The position of a congressional leader is thus more fragile and vulnerable than in the 1960s and it is perhaps striking that two of the most publicized congressional scandals of recent years have involved leaders in the House of Representatives, Speakers Wright and Gingrich.

Jim Wright and Newt Gingrich are very different in their political outlooks and personal philosophies but both possessed aspirations, even visions, not normally associated with the role of Speaker of the House. If Congress has often deferred to the president in foreign-policy matters, the House of Representatives has usually played second fiddle to the Senate because of the latter's war-declaring, appointment-confirming and treaty-ratifying powers. Yet, in the vacuum of US foreign policy in central America which followed the revelations of the Reagan administration's involvement in the Iran–Contra scandal, it was Speaker Jim Wright who took it upon himself to try to fill the void by attempting to broker his own Nicaraguan peace plan by having discussions with leaders of foreign governments. This unprecedented initiative was not well received by the Reagan White House or by the Republicans in Congress who regarded his action as improper, as a usurpation of power. The long-standing Democratic control of the House had long been a source of frustration to congressional Republicans, and the spectacle of a Democrat Speaker appointing himself as the architect of American foreign policy was too much to bear.

If Jim Wright was thought to have tried to extend the role of the Speaker beyond its customary bounds, Newt Gingrich, the first

Republican Speaker in forty years, went even further by attempting to wrest the policy initiative from President Clinton and by exercising firm control over his Republican colleagues in the House of Representatives. His attempt to make the Congress and, more particularly, the House of Representatives the central driving force of American politics was not designed to endear Gingrich to his Democrat opponents. He was already held in low regard because of the extreme nature of his views and his role in the Jim Wright scandal, but now it seemed Gingrich was intent on usurping the first Democrat in the White House for more than a decade.

In 1989, Jim Wright was forced to resign his post as Speaker after only two years in office. Thirty-four years of congressional service had come to an ignominious end. Similarly, after two years in office, Speaker Gingrich found himself struggling for his political life. He retained his post after the 1996 elections but quickly became the first Speaker to be formally reprimanded and fined by the House of Representatives. The fact that this vote to reprimand was supported by most of his Republican colleagues is a measure of how far Gingrich has fallen. Gingrich's political future is uncertain, his presidential aspirations are 'on hold', and some commentators regard him as a spent force. These two cases of high-profile individuals embroiled in scandals which destroyed or damaged their political careers will complement the discussions of collective scandals in Congress.

What all these examples, individual and collective, have in common are issues of legitimacy and propriety. The legitimacy of receiving gifts and favours from constituents, the propriety of deriving inflated sums from 'books' and other outside sources, the legitimacy of exploiting institutional privileges and apparent loopholes in codes of conduct, and the propriety of pressurizing officials in exchange for campaign contributions or of accepting money from lobbyists. In almost all the cases, the members of Congress accused of scandalous behaviour protested that they had been wrongly accused, made scapegoats for the sins of others or were the victims of aggressive partizanship. On their own accounts, it seems that the behaviour under attack was, in fact, perfectly proper but deliberately misunderstood or, if questionable, was so widespread as to make their scandals cases of victimization. The fact remains that 'more members of Congress have been investigated and subjected to sanctions for ethical misconduct in the past decade and a half than in the entire previous history of the institution'.[7] It will be discussed later whether this is indicative of a massive upsurge in unethical and poten-tially scandalous behaviour in recent times or whether behaviour which was once conventional and acceptable is now regarded as unethical and scandalous. What cannot be denied is that, measured in terms of media coverage, congressional investigations, criminal charges and public opinion, Congress is a chronically scandal-prone institution.

The particular scandals considered here are, of course, not the only scandals that have occurred in the past twenty years, but they are important ones in terms of their political consequences and the insights they offer into the role of scandals in congressional politics. As with the presidential examples, scandals involving private or personal matters have been disregarded. It is perhaps worth noting that, as public and media expectations of official conduct have risen, standards regarding private behaviour and morality seem to have become less strict. This applies not only to heterosexual behaviour – the concern about Rocke-feller's divorce in the 1960s and the lack of concern about Dole's in the 1990s – but also to homosexual behaviour. Thus, Representative Barney Frank was not only able to 'come out' in the 1980s without suffering adverse electoral consequences but he also survived a public scandal concerning his employment of a former lover who ran a male prostitute service from Frank's congressional office.

The congressional scandals discussed here occurred in the post-Watergate period but, as noted above, concern about scandalous behaviour in Congress had grown, both internally and externally, since at least the Bobby Baker scandal in the 1960s. The post-Watergate congressional elections saw almost a landslide for the Democrats who had large majorities in both chambers but, in 1977, a group of Californian Democrats in the House of Representatives found themselves under investigation for receiving money from a lobbyist working for the government of South Korea.

The so-called 'Koreagate' scandal raised some key issues which have surfaced again and again in subsequent scandals. The lobbyist, Tongsun Park, was ostensibly involved in the rice trade with the United States but he also had links with the South Korean intelligence agencies. His role was to cultivate as many friends as possible in the US Congress. Tongsun Park gave evidence to the House Ethics Committee that he had given gifts and made campaign contributions to thirty present or former congressmen. Park was indicted in 1977 on charges of conspiring to bribe public officials but, through an intergovernmental arrangement, the charges were never prosecuted in exchange for Park agreeing to give testimony about whom had been paid, how much and in what form.

It emerged that in some cases the payments had begun long before Carter's election and, in one case, as early as 1967. Although at one point the allegation seemed to be that nearly 10 per cent of congressmen had received payments, the eventual outcome was that, in October 1978, the House formally reprimanded three current members, John McFall, Edward Roybal and Charles Wilson, all Democrats from California. In congressional language, a reprimand is more serious than a rebuke but less serious than a vote of censure and, of course, much less serious than expulsion. One former congressman, Richard Hanna, also a Democrat from California, faced criminal charges as a co-conspirator with Park and received a prison sentence.

In dealing with the serving congressmen, the House seemed to make a distinction between the attempt to offer payments as a bribe, which is illegal, and the motives and the understanding of those in receipt of payments. If the members were found guilty of bribery, the result would most likely have been expulsion or at least censure. But the House took the view that the payments were received as campaign contributions or simply as goodwill gifts. In the view of the House they were reprimanded for misusing ostensible campaign contributions and for not disclosing their receipt. In the case of Roybal, he was also found to have been less than frank in his answers.

What started with criminal indictments and the apparent bribery of several dozen congressmen ended less spectacularly. Both Roybal and Wilson, who had been reprimanded only a month earlier, were re-elected to the House in November 1978. This suggested to some that their behaviour was not truly scandalous because no one was shocked by it, least of all their electorates. It seems that, up to the late 1970s, it was widely understood that lobbyists plied members of Congress with gifts, trips and campaign contributions as part of their effort to ensure good will and the need to ensure access to legislators. From the congressmen's perspective, such gifts and donations were effectively 'perks' of the job and it was unthinkable that relatively modest sums could actually bribe members by encouraging them to change their votes.

Koreagate seemed to lack the specificity necessary to generate authentic public indignation. To adapt the Watergate question, 'what did the congressmen do and when?' The receipt of the money without evidence of actual specific reciprocation or at least the promise of some

KING ALFRED'S COLLEGE
LIBRARY

exceptional or unusual political response suggested a lack of judgement rather than criminal intent. At least some of the media indignation focused less on the greed or gullibility of the congressmen involved as on the actions of a supposedly friendly country trying to bankroll members of Congress. Koreagate thus had diplomatic implications as well as institutional consequences.

The dust of Koreagate had hardly settled when the next alleged bribery scandal involving Congress erupted. If Koreagate was contentious because of the involvement of a foreign government, the Abscam scandal, which ran from 1980 to 1982, was contentious because of the role played by the FBI. In this case, criminal prosecutions supplemented internal disciplinary action by Congress, and the scandal received extensive press and television coverage. It was a scandal with the sort of bizarre elements that catch the attention of both the media and the public. It began as a sort of 'sting' operation designed to trap public officials who were suspected of corruption. The plan involved FBI agents, posing as an Arab sheikh, 'Kambir Abdul Rahman', and his entourage, offering bribes to members of both House and Senate in exchange for explicit offers of help with resolving supposed immigration and business problems. It is known as Abscam because it was an 'Arab scam', a scam being a confidence trick. It is alleged, however, that President Carter took exception on racial grounds to the term and subsequent official accounts suggest that Abscam actually stood for 'Abdul scam'. Whatever the derivation of its popular label, it eventually resulted in criminal convictions for seven members of Congress, as well as state and city officials in Pennsylvania and New Jersey.

There is no doubt that a number of members of Congress were alarmed by the FBI's commitment and the resources it invested in the Abscam operation. Over a two-year period, some 100 FBI agents were engaged in an undercover investigation of legislative corruption. One who gave voice to his concerns was Senator Alan Cranston, who commented: 'If the FBI is allowed to do what it did, that presents a dire danger to the separation of powers'.[8] If there was concern expressed by the legislature about the scandalmongering of an agency of the executive branch, there was also an attempt to mount a legal defence based on the notion of entrapment. This involves the idea that law-enforcement agencies should not themselves engage in conduct likely to cause crimes to be committed which would not otherwise be committed. Most commonly, the defence has been used where police have posed as prostitutes or drug dealers but, in Abscam, the argument was that the offer of bribes by FBI agents constituted an integral part of an offence which would not have happened without such an offer. After exhausting the appeal process, the courts rejected the entrapment defence offered by the convicted members of Congress.

The criminal outcome of Abscam was the conviction and imprisonment of one US Senator and six members of the House of Representatives. All seven guilty men had previously failed to win re-election or had been expelled or had resigned from Congress. Six of the guilty men were, as in the Koreagate scandal, Democrats: Senator Harrison Williams (NJ), Representatives Frank Thompson (NJ), Michael Myers and Raymond Lederer (Pennsylvania), John Murphy (NY) and John Jenrette (South Carolina). The one Republican involved was Representative Richard Kelly (Florida). A further congressman, Representative John Murtha (Pennsylvania), was also indicted but not prosecuted because he gave evidence against Murphy and Thompson. In October 1980, Michael 'Ozzie' Myers achieved the distinction of becoming the first member of the House to be expelled since 1861. This suggested that congressional attitudes to bribery and the scandal associated with it had undergone a sea change, in that only a few years earlier, the House had declined to expel a Californian Republican, Andrew Hinshaw, who had also been convicted of accepting a bribe. Admittedly, Hinshaw's conviction related to conduct before he was elected to the House. By the time those implicated in Abscam had been convicted, the House was ready to show the public that it would not tolerate such explicit flouting of congressional rules and the criminal law. It is important to appreciate here the political context of the period with the passage of major ethics reform – the Ethics in Government Act – only two years earlier. Standards of official conduct were high on everyone's political agenda and those caught in the headlights of media attention were not likely to receive lenient treatment.

The Abscam defendants were, in one sense, victims of a radical and relatively sudden change in the ethical climate brought about by Watergate, a variety of legislative measures, and a tightening-up in the rules of Congress itself. The behaviour in Abscam might well have been regarded as improper in the 1960s but, the 1980s, there was a political imperative driving the ethics process in Congress. The FBI operation involved extensive secret filming of some of the members of Congress involved, and this demonstration of official greed disgusted public opinion. One congressman, John Jenrette, was heard to declare 'I've got larceny in my blood',[9] and, in the face of such evidence, most congressmen deemed it politically prudent not to give any public appearance of support for the Abscam defendants.

The only senator trapped in the operation, Senator Harrison Williams, had previously earned respect for conscientious work in Congress over more than twenty years and he insisted that, while he had accepted mining stock from the 'sheikh', he 'never intended to do anything that would bring dishonour to the Senate'[10] but, in the eyes of Congress and in the court of public opinion, he was judged to have been acting for personal financial gain and to have been motivated by greed. Contrary to the advice of the ethics committee's special counsel, the Senate postponed disciplining Williams until the legal appeal process was completed. The well-respected Senator Alan Cranston, who was himself to become notorious during the Keating Five scandal, led an effort to censure rather than expel Williams. No senator had ever been expelled from the Senate for corruption but the publicity of Abscam and the stigma of criminal conviction made Williams's position extremely precarious. On 11 March 1982, Senator Williams resigned from the Senate just before the Senate was to vote on his expulsion. His resignation had the dual benefit of avoiding the notoriety of being the first senator to suffer expulsion and the not inconsiderable consideration of preserving his pension. It did not, however, prevent him from being sent to prison.

Abscam illustrates that clear and explicit evidence of personal corruption involving members of Congress leads to political scandals of such proportions that political survival is almost impossible. The weight of public disapproval, media condemnation and rejection by institutional colleagues is too great to endure. But as Koreagate suggests, and later scandals like the Keating Five and the House Banking scandal confirm, convincing evidence of corruption is rare. Most scandals in Congress and in the executive branch are not so black and white or clear cut.

Bribery is notoriously difficult to prove. The law is neither precise nor consistent, and prosecutors usually prefer to find alternative charges which are easier to prove. In law, bribery requires all the following elements: a public official; a corrupt intention on the part of the person offering the bribe; a benefit to the official; a relationship between a thing of value and some official act; and an intention to influence the carrying-out of an official act.[11] There is a related criminal offence of accepting an illegal gratuity which demands a lower standard of criminal intent.

It is, of course, possible for one person to offer what he or she regards as a bribe with the intent of influencing an official act, but for a member of Congress to receive it without understanding that intention or intending himself that it would influence his official action. In such cases, a charge of attempted bribery may be laid against the party offering the bribe without charging the recipient. One useful distinction between a bribe and an illegal gratuity is that a bribe is intended to motivate some future official act whereas a gratuity is a reward for past service. As Thompson notes, 'A bribe says "please" and a gratuity says "thank you"'.[12]

Official conduct which does not meet legal standards of criminal intent may still be regarded by the public and the media as improper and therefore generate a scandal. But there are often problems in identifying exactly who is responsible for what as well as defining the limits of proper and improper behaviour. The case of the Keating Five illustrates these difficulties very well in that there was widely perceived to be a scandal but explaining exactly what the improper behaviour was proved a challenge to the ethics committee. While the link between personal corruption and scandal is relatively straightforward, scandals associated with the development and implementation of public policies are less easy to characterize. With any public policy in the American political system, there are always controversies about authorship and control. Where policies are successful, the President and Congress compete to claim credit and, when they go wrong, blame-avoidance and transfer become political imperatives.

It was widely agreed among the parties and political institutions that there was an urgent need to reform the law regulating the Savings and Loan industry. Savings and Loan institutions, or thrifts as they are often called, had developed to provide loans to enable individuals to buy homes, usually at fixed and relatively low rates of interest. Changes in the financial sector and rapid rates of inflation made the thrifts look anachronistic, and it was agreed that various restrictions on their lending power be removed to allow them to compete in the financial market. Whatever the motives for this piece of deregulation, it went sadly wrong and many Savings and Loans expanded rapidly on a speculative basis and then collapsed. In 1989, official estimates of the financial bailout for the insolvent thrifts were placed at $200 billion over the next decade. More recent estimates have been pitched at over $300 billion.[13]

Faced with a policy disaster of this magnitude, there was a public and media need to apportion blame, to find scapegoats. In one sense, the Keating Five were unlucky and unfortunate in that they came to be associated with 'the biggest failure in what came to be the most costly financial scandal in American history'.[14] In consequence they symbolized the financial mess known as the Savings and Loan scandal.

In 1984, Charles Keating Jr had bought Lincoln Savings and Loan based in California. Keating was the owner of a construction company based in Arizona and, like many other similar entrepreneurs, he shifted Lincoln's assets from home loans to more speculative investments and construction projects. He used his lawyers to stave off inquiries from state regulators who believed that Lincoln was violating a number of financial and accounting regulations. Keating used his political connections to lobby for further deregulation, and he also campaigned against Edwin Gray, the chairman of the Federal Home Loan Bank (FHLB), which regulated the Savings and Loan industry.

On 2 April 1987, four United States Senators, three Democrat and one Republican, met in a senator's office with Chairman Edwin Gray to discuss the FHLB's investigation of the Lincoln Savings and Loan. The meeting had been arranged by Democratic Senator, Don Riegle, and Gray was advised not to bring any staff with him. In the event, Riegle himself was unable to attend, but four senators were present: Dennis DeConcini (Arizona); Alan Cranston (California); John Glenn (Ohio); and the lone Republican, John McCain (Arizona). The senators asked why the investigation was taking so long and, on Gray's account, proposed a deal whereby if Gray relaxed certain rules, Keating would move Lincoln Savings and Loan back into traditional home loans.

Gray realized that four senators in one meeting about one Savings and Loan was unusual and he later reported that he was intimidated by this show of force. He claimed that he did not know very much about the Lincoln case and suggested they talk with the FHLB examiners in San Francisco who were currently handling the case. The senators followed up this suggestion and, a week later, another meeting took place with all five senators present, together with four regulators from the San Francisco office. At this meeting it was suggested they were harassing Keating but, as the meeting progressed, the examiners revealed that they were about to make a criminal referral against Lincoln. Criminal referrals do not automatically imply guilt but they might be thought sufficiently alarming to make a prudent senator act with great caution. In fact, Riegle and McCain withdrew from the fray and had no further contact with Keating, Gray or the San Francisco examiners. McCain had already broken off relations with Keating because Keating had called McCain a wimp for not agreeing to put more pressure on the FHLB board. Senator Glenn arranged for Keating to lunch with Speaker Jim Wright in January 1988 but otherwise played no further part in advancing Keating's interests.

But despite the effective withdrawal of McCain, Riegle and Glenn as well as the criminal referral warning from the bank examiners, Senators DeConcini and Cranston continued to intervene actively on Keating's behalf. In 1989, Cranston approached bank regulators at least six times in a two-month period, including an early morning phone call to the home of a member of the FHLB Board. DeConcini, who had lobbied on Keating's behalf for years, also made calls to both state and federal regulators about the future of Lincoln Savings and Loan. Partly as a result of the senatorial pressure, the investigations of Keating and Lincoln were moved from the allegedly too-vigorous regulators in San Francisco to the central office in Washington. This move contributed to the delay in actually getting to grips with Lincoln's financial practices and position.

In 1989, Lincoln Savings and Loan finally collapsed, and the American taxpayer picked up a bill of more than two billion dollars. Charles Keating was subsequently imprisoned on fraud and racketeering charges. The Keating Five senators received a total of $1.3 million from Keating in campaign contributions, with $850,000 going to Cranston, mostly in 1987 and 1988 when he was actively helping Keating. But these headline figures, which helped give the scandal added momentum, actually concealed more than they revealed. The headline numbers revealed nothing about when the money was received or in what form. The headlines also implied that there was something improper about the payments but they were all within the legal limits. The money that Cranston received was not primarily money directed for his own campaign but rather what is known as 'soft money' intended for party-building and voter-registration projects.

Riegle and DeConcini had solicited contributions from Keating while intervening with regulators on his behalf. Riegle received $78,000 and DeConcini $48,000 in direct campaign contributions. Ironically, the senators least involved in intervening on behalf of Keating, McCain and Glenn, received the largest amounts in campaign and political-action-committee funds but, in both cases, they received them long before they became actively involved in helping Keating.

While the Keating Five scandal 'is the most well-publicized instance of influence-peddling to stave off scrutiny of thrift activities, it is only part of a larger pattern'.[15] Opinion polls suggest that the Savings and Loan scandal was the scandal that provoked most public concern, and they also indicate that most Americans believe that the scandalous behaviour of the Keating Five is typical of the behaviour of members of Congress.[16] Clearly it was a very different sort of scandal from Abscam in that none of the Keating Five sought personally to enrich themselves by abusing their official positions. The question that needed answering was, if this was a scandal (and the public and media certainly thought it was), what exactly had the Keating Five done wrong?

The Senate Ethics Committee took nine months of investigation and seven weeks of hearings to come up with the answers. The problem is that the American electoral system requires candidates to solicit campaign contributions and, once in office, constituents expect elected office-holders to attend to their problems. Thus, if the two key activities of election fund-raising and constituency service are legitimate and even desirable, what was there in the way these functions were performed by the Keating Five that provoked a major scandal? The conclusions they eventually reached was that four of the five had displayed 'insensitivity' and 'poor judgement' and were formally rebuked by the Senate. Riegle and DeConcini were presumably more insensitive and displayed even poorer judgement than Glenn and McCain because they were rebuked in harsher terms and both retired from the Senate when their terms expired.

The scapegoat for the Keating Five scandal was Senator Cranston. Having dealt with four senators in February 1991, it was not until November that the Ethics Committee reported to the Senate that Cranston had 'violated established norms of behaviour in the Senate'.[17] It found the contributions and services to be 'substantially linked' through an 'impermissible pattern of conduct'[18] but, perhaps for the legal reasons discussed above, they did not find that Cranston was motivated by any corrupt intent. In effect, the committee said that Cranston's conduct was not corrupt but to any reasonable person it could very well appear so. Cranston was reprimanded by the Senate for behaving in such a way as to give an appearance of corruption. Cranston formally accepted the reprimand rather than risk an even stronger resolution being put to the vote. But Cranston repeated his innocence, rejected the appearance standard employed by the Committee, and insisted that he had behaved no differently from most of his fellow senators.[19]

The Keating Five scandal had some unusual features: five senators combining to exert pressure, and a businessman lavishing large sums of money on legislators whose political views were at odds with his own. The general public and the media commentators found it hard to follow the distinctions drawn between the five senators and the choice of Cranston as the scapegoat seemed both odd and too easy. Not only was Cranston a long-standing advocate of campaign reform but he was ill with cancer and had already announced his decision not to stand for re-election. The pressure of political imperatives in the Ethics Committee's judgements is confirmed by their rejection of their special counsel's recommendation to drop McCain from the inquiry. This rejection seems largely motivated by the Democrat majority's determination to have at least one Republican Senator share the political responsibility for the savings and loan scandal. The broader Savings and Loan scandal was simply too complex and the responsibilities too blurred to identify those responsible, and the Keating Five scandal provided a convenient means for Congress to demonstrate that it was doing something about those responsible for this financial disaster.

The reality is that Congress had a collective responsibility for the Savings and Loan scandal because in 1986 it failed to pass legislation which was designed to ensure more effective regulation and control of thrifts. Many members of Congress 'used their power of the purse to try to get regulators to go easy on individual Savings and Loans belonging to constituents and campaign contributors'.[20] Among those involved in the 1986 blocking actions were Representative Jim Wright and Senator David Pryor, the latter was a member of the Senate Ethics Committee which later sat in judgement on the Keating Five. In such circumstances, it is unsurprising that the public is inclined to believe that most politicians engage in scandalous behaviour.

The profound levels of public distrust and cynicism account for the severe public reaction to the so-called House Banking scandal in 1991 which contributed in substantial part to the large turnover in the House of Representatives in the 1992 congressional elections.[21] This scandal was founded on the deep-rooted popular resentment at elected politicians granting themselves privileges not available to the general public. The furore over the House Bank suggests that even the hint of scandal can be extremely damaging to legislative careers even where the alleged improprieties are trivial.

Since the early 1950s the House Bank had been in the habit of honouring cheques written by members who were overdrawn. The fact that it did so was not widely known to the public. In September 1991, the General Accounting Office reported that members had written more than 8,000 bad cheques in a twelve-month period. The report engendered a chorus of critical responses, and the Speaker announced that the bank would close and an ethics committee investigation would be held. The investigation found that more than 300 current and former members, a large majority of them Democrats, had written bad cheques. After initial resistance, the names of those involved were released. The ethics committee recommended no further action, and a special counsel who carried out a lengthy investigation decided against bringing any criminal charges.

But while the institutional reaction was that this was 'much ado about nothing', the public response was totally different. Most Americans thought it was serious and it ranked ahead of Iran–Contra and only behind the Savings and Loan scandal in many peoples' estimates of importance.[22] Public reaction was so strong that involvement in the scandal 'increased the likelihood that one would retire from the House, be denied renomination and perform more poorly in the general election'.[23]

The facts of the scandal were not well understood. The bad cheques were drawn on the pool of House salaries and did not involve any public subsidy or taxpayer loss. But the public believed overwhelmingly that House members had broken the law, and half thought that the overdrawn cheques were being met by the taxpayer.[24] If the scandal served to strengthen institutional distrust, it was also used to seek partisan advantage. The preponderance of Democrats in the ranks of bad-cheque writers was exploited by Republicans 'to illustrate the possibility that long-time control of the legislature by one political party could tempt members of that party to use a public institution for private gain'.[25]

One major study of congressional ethics concluded that 'As measured by the size of personal gain or the risk to the public purse, the House Bank problem must rank as one of the least serious scandals in congressional history'.[26] Yet this 'least serious' of scandals led to more than forty members of the House, who were particularly tainted by the scandal, retiring or facing defeat in the 1992 elections.

All the congressional scandals discussed thus far have had a group identity. None has involved a single senator or representative acting alone or in some unique way. While individual legislators have been subject to specific discipline by Congress or faced particular charges in the criminal courts, their actions were in some sense collective in that they acted together or were aware that others were acting in a similar fashion. This sense of collective action militates against notions of individual culpability and encourages legislators to see their conduct as legitimate whether that involves gifts from lobbyists, campaign contributions from constituents or enjoying free overdraft facilities. It was noted in the discussion of the Bank scandal that the political consequences of the conduct in question seemed disproportionate to its seriousness. It was further noted that partisan considerations helped to fuel the scandal and give the Republicans an opportunity to seize the moral high ground.

The final examples of congressional scandal discussed in this chapter are of a rather different character to the collective scandals discussed above. The scandals which centred around Democrat Speaker Jim Wright[27] and Republican Speaker Newt Gingrich[28] raise a number of other issues and considerations. In these cases, the focus of public and media attention was on an individual and not a group. It was not merely a question of numbers but, more importantly, the identities of the individuals at the centre of the storm. These were not junior freshmen unversed in the ways of Congress but certainly the most powerful and senior figures in the House of Representatives and probably in the Congress as a whole. The scandals that engulfed Jim Wright and came close to destroying Newt Gingrich had different origins and motivations. They had much more to do with the control, use and organization of political power and much less to do with private greed. In these cases we see more clearly than ever before the emergence of scandal as a potent weapon in partisan politics, a club with which to beat your political opponents. From the late 1980s onwards, scandal became the political weapon of choice. Politicians began systematically to use scandal allegations to achieve victories over rivals who had defeated them at the ballot box.

As the role of scandal allegations within Congress has developed, so has the institutional context in which they are made. Congress changed dramatically in the years after Watergate, with major reforms of the committee and subcommittee structures, the erosion of seniority and a substantial expansion of staff. In one politically incorrect phrase, everyone in Congress was a chief and no one was an indian. In the majority party, everyone chaired something, everyone had a piece of turf and everyone had lots of staff. This move towards, in one sense, democratization, exacerbated the task of leadership in Congress. What junior members saw as democratization, congressional leaders and President Carter saw as fragmentation and incoherence. One counter-vailing response was to strengthen and broaden the power of the Speaker over the referral of bills, the timetables for committees, and the creation of *ad hoc* committees, and to appoint the Rules Committee. Such reforms served both to increase the Speaker's status and power and to enhance party control at the expense of committees and those that lead them. More members enjoyed chairing committees or sub-committees but the power and autonomy of the committees were reduced.

The election and re-election of a popular Republican president in the 1980s forced a further reappraisal. Reagan's policy agenda and budgetary constraints limited the scope for congressional activism, and the Demo-crats forged a closer unity in their adversity. The increase in ideological and organizational cohesion in the majority party further strengthened the powers of the party leaders in general and the Speaker in particular. By the time Jim Wright became Speaker in 1987 the office had been transformed both from what it was a decade earlier and from what it had been for most of the twentieth century. Speaker Wright 'assumed the mantle of leader of the opposition frequently appearing on television to reply to presidential messages and publicize alternative Democratic policy proposals'.[29] Thus, the modern Speaker of the House has become a powerful political actor in the American system of government and, so long as he retains the support of his party members, the Speaker can set much of the agenda of the House and become the dominant con-gressional player in the important budget process.

The political context when Wright became Speaker was especially propitious. Not only had the power of the office grown considerably but he was backed by a relatively well-disciplined Democratic majority in the House. He enjoyed the added advantage of facing a once-popular and successful Republican President who had now been seriously weak-ened by the revelations of the Iran–Contra scandal. It was noted earlier that Wright attempted in an unprecedented fashion to use his office to launch a foreign-policy initiative intended to end the war in Nicaragua. Such an initiative was extraordinary at the time but unthinkable a decade earlier.

Jim Wright had his own style as Speaker which was different from that of his predecessor, Tip O'Neill, and that of his successor, Tom

Foley. O'Neill solicited members' opinions before deciding how to act while Foley was more conciliatory, even deferential, to the chairs of committees and was perceived by many as weak. Jim Wright attempted to be a leader in the sense that he assumed that the initiative lay with him and he sought to bind House Democrats to his decisions. Compared to Foley, Wright was autocratic and abrasive and he had no time and little consideration for the minority Republicans in the House. His leadership style was to have important political consequences when he became the subject of a major scandal.

Wright's aggressive, assertive style of leadership caused tensions within his own party and fierce animosity from the Republicans. He was something of a political 'loner' without substantial personal support from members of the House, and this lack of support was to prove crucial when he came under attack for alleged misconduct. He had no reservoir of support to draw on to help him ride out the attacks of the Republicans and the charges of the House ethics committee. To adapt a familiar Watergate phrase, he was left 'twisting in the wind'.

One of Wright's weaknesses was an ability to unite seemingly disparate forces against him. It is widely accepted that a relatively junior conservative Republican, Newt Gingrich, was largely responsible for orchestrating the attacks on Wright which led to the House ethics committee's investigations. Gingrich's role was certainly important in increasing the political temperature and momentum but it is less widely appreciated that Wright's conduct had also alienated the liberal interest group, *Common Cause*, which wrote formally to the House ethics committee demanding an investigation of Wright. There is little doubt, however, that Gingrich saw an opportunity to launch a personal crusade against Wright which, if successful, would enhance Gingrich's standing and profile, bring down the most important Democrat in Congress and, indirectly, smear with a reputation for corruption Democrats in both houses. The stakes were therefore very high, and Gingrich deployed his now-familiar energy and zeal in alerting colleagues, the media and the public to Wright's alleged misconduct.

In 1988, a special counsel began what was to prove a seven-month investigation of Wright and, in April 1989, his 270-page report was issued. The House ethics committee began proceeding on five allegations of misconduct because, it asserted, 'there is reason to believe such violations occurred'.[30] A somewhat surprising observation for a quasi-judicial body that had not yet heard Wright's defence. The charges against Wright included receiving income from a book deal which violated House rules on honorariums and outside income; exercising undue influence with the FHLB Board and its chairman, Edwin Gray (the same charge as the Keating Five); receiving gifts from a constituent, George Mallick, with a direct interest in legislation pending before Congress; and profiting improperly from an oil-well deal. These were the broad charges but, once the committee broke them down into each discrete violation of House rules, it came up with a total of sixty-nine counts. The media and public impact of such a large number of alleged violations was considerable.

Given that the Keating Five were later rebuked or reprimanded for their interventions with the FHLB, it is perhaps surprising that, two years earlier, the House ethics committee dismissed the charge of improper intervention. The special counsel had devoted a third of his report to this charge and concluded that Wright had sought to persuade the FHLB both to change certain staff who were being unco-operative with Wright's constituents and, in contravention of Board rules, to meet an individual who was legally barred from operating any government-insured organization. In one case, Wright apparently sought the removal of a tough regulator on the grounds that he was homosexual. According to the chair of the FHLB, Wright had indicated that he would hold up certain legislation necessary to the Board's work unless he got co-operation. But the full horror of the Savings and Loan scandal was not yet apparent, and the House ethics committee concluded that, while Wright may have been 'intemperate',[31] he was simply looking after his constituents.

It was the book deal and his relationship with businessman, George Mallick, that undermined Wright. The book deal involved selling in bulk to lobbyists and other groups, and a royalty rate of 55 per cent which was thought sufficiently unusual to cast doubt on the whole enterprise. As far as Mallick was concerned, Wright allegedly received some $145,000 worth of gifts and benefits, and the committee concluded that he 'had failed in his duty to exercise reasonable care to avoid even the appearance of impropriety'.[32]

Wright tried to argue that the book deal was a legitimate loophole and that Mallick's interests in legislation were no greater than those of many other business people. But the pressure on him was considerable, and his public standing was further undermined by fresh scandal allegations involving one of his top aides. In early May 1989, it was alleged that Wright had used his influence in the mid-1970s to ensure that his son-in-law's brother received a lenient sentence for a horrific crime of violence, and that this same individual, John Mack, had subsequently become Wright's top aide in Congress. On 31 May 1989, under the weight of the House charges and the Mack scandal, Jim Wright resigned as Speaker of the House of Representatives.

Gingrich's victory was complete. Shortly before Wright resigned, his expected successor, Tony Coelho, resigned because of allegations about improper conduct involving insider-dealing and questionable fund-raising methods. Coelho truncated his scandal by resigning immediately and not waiting for the laborious investigation and adjudication processes of the House. In any event, the House Democrat leadership had been destroyed and Newt Gingrich's prominent role in manipulating the press and keeping the scandals going was warmly appreciated by his Republican colleagues. The House Republicans had long regarded themselves as an oppressed minority, treated with contempt by the seemingly permanent Democrat majority, and revenge was sweet. The House Democrats, of course, took a very different view of events and, while they were not dedicated supporters of Jim Wright, they took great exception to Gingrich's politically motivated crusade against him. Newt Gingrich rose to political prominence on a wave of scandal, and it was to be expected that his political opponents would seek to turn his own weapon, multiple allegations of scandal, against him.

Gingrich's success, if such it can be called, has been to politicize the ethics issue in Congress. The partizanship that had characterized the handling of the Bobby Baker scandal in the 1960s had temporarily given way to a formal, bipartizan approach, but Gingrich's successful assault on Wright confirmed that, in Congress, bipartizanship is an unnatural act. The bipartizan machinery and procedures remain in place but the political gains to be made by making scandalous allegations have been demonstrated to be so large that partizanship of an increasingly bitter kind now dominates the congressional approach to scandal.

When the Republicans swept to power in the House in the 1994 elections, Newt Gingrich became the first Republican Speaker for forty years. Many Republicans believed that they owed much of their success to Gingrich, and he was given power to choose the chairs of committees, to shape committee assignments and, in general, to increase the authority of the Speaker. Gingrich went even further than Wright in assuming responsibility for media relations and, rather like a prime minister in a

parliamentary system, he began demanding prime-time slots on television to address the American people. Newt Gingrich had arrived on the
national political stage and he was determined to play the major role.
He marshalled his Republican troops to ensure disciplined majorities for
his 'Contract with America', and he set out to challenge Democrat
President Bill Clinton for control of the national agenda.

Complaints had been made that Gingrich was using improperly his
congressional payroll for political purposes but no action was taken
against him by the House ethics committee.[33] Further complaints to the
ethics committee came, in September 1994, from Ben Jones, his Democrat opponent in the 1994 election. But once Gingrich became Speaker,
the floodgates opened. Jones filed a complaint in January 1995. In
February, separate complaints were received from a group of Democratic representatives (Patricia Schroeder, Harry Johnston and Cynthia
McKinney) and from a public-interest group, the Congress Accountability Project. By then, the House Democratic Whip, David Bonior,
got into his stride and he made separate complaints against Gingrich in
March, May and December. The allegations against Gingrich have taken
a variety of forms including his relations with GOPAC (a political action
committee), improper use of staff, his video-taped university course, his
links with cable television stations, tax violations and a questionable
book deal with HarperCollins. Some of these complaints were dismissed
by the ethics committee in December 1995 but, in regard to the book
deal, the committee wrote to Gingrich questioning 'the appropriateness
of what some could describe as an attempt by you to capitalize on your
office'. It added, 'At a minimum, this creates the impression of exploiting
one's office for personal gain. Such a perception is especially troubling
when it pertains to the office of the Speaker of the House, a constitutional
office requiring the highest standards of ethical behaviour.'[34]

The Democrats had been demanding the appointment of a special
counsel from the time of the Jones complaint in 1994 but the Republicans
resisted for as long as they could. In the Jim Wright case, a special
counsel had been appointed within a few weeks, and Democrats and
Republicans were mindful of the damage his report had done to Wright.
The Republicans claimed that the Democrats' demands were simply
politically motivated partisan revenge for what happened to Wright.
The Democrats claimed that the Republicans' view of scandal had
changed now they were in a majority in the House. Where once they
had been zealous in their desire to expose wrongdoing to the public

gaze, they were now motivated by a desire to protect the Speaker, their Speaker, and they were prepared to abuse the House ethics procedures to do so.

The ethics committee has equal representation of Democrats and Republicans and therefore the party pressing for the appointment of a special counsel has to be able to persuade at least one member of the opposing party to support their demand. The media coverage of the fights over the appointment had been extensive and there was a growing concern that Gingrich and the Republicans had something to hide. The dismissal of some complaints still left others unanswered. There was residual concern about the 1994 book deal[35] and the committee found that Gingrich had violated certain rules and misused floor privileges. Although no disciplinary action was recommended, the committee at last agreed to appoint a special counsel, James Cole, in December 1995.

By 1996, Gingrich's political stock had begun to fall, partly perhaps because of the seemingly endless allegations of unethical conduct, but also because he had handled the budget struggle with President Clinton ineptly and the Republicans had received most of the blame for shutting down the government.[36] Gingrich had presented himself as the man of the hour who would lead a transformation of the United States but, in reality, President Clinton had seized the initiative and regained control of political events. Gingrich's popularity plummeted and he soon became the most unpopular politician in a country where all politicians are unpopular. Even his allies thought he was prone to mistakes and, in September 1996, the Republican chair of the House ethics committee, Nancy Johnson, observed a 'continuing pattern of lax administration and poor judgement'.[37] More ominously still, the ethics committee voted unanimously to expand James Cole's investigation of Gingrich's college course to examine whether the information supplied by the Speaker was accurate, complete and reliable.

In December 1996, the special counsel submitted his report to the ethics subcommittee. The press was rife with speculation about its content and the consequences for Speaker Gingrich. On 19 December Gingrich's ethics lawyer resigned, saying that he had not submitted any information to the ethics committee without Gingrich's approval. Some Republicans tried again to shift responsibility away from the Speaker by claiming that any inaccurate information given to the committee was his lawyer's responsibility. But, on 21 December 1996, the committee released a twenty-two-page *Statement of Alleged Violations*, the committee equivalent of an indictment. The carefully balanced document concluded: 'Gingrich used an army of charitable organizations to subsidize his partizan political activities; and that he submitted "inaccurate, incomplete and unreliable" information to the panel about the connection between the college course and GOPAC'.[38]

Despite his previous and frequent denials of wrongdoing, Gingrich sought to bring proceedings to a swift conclusion. To the surprise of many press commentators, Gingrich immediately accepted the *Statement of Alleged Violations* but he and his Republican colleagues went on to argue that the violations were unintentional and involved 'arcane' areas of tax law. In effect, they claimed he had failed to consult the right kind of lawyer to resolve the tax issues.

The Gingrich scandal then moved into another phase. The question now was what the political consequences for Gingrich would be. House Republican Conference rules prohibit a Representative who has been censured from holding a leadership post and it therefore became a political imperative for Republicans to ensure that Gingrich was only rebuked or reprimanded because anything more serious would prevent him from serving another term as Speaker. They also sought to accelerate the process by which the full ethics committee would consider what penalties to impose on Gingrich. Democrats, on the other hand, wanted to prolong the sentencing exercise.

These Republican tactics were to provoke further press headlines, with Democrats and Republicans swapping allegations about improper conduct and abuses of the ethics process. Democrats were relishing the prospect of Gingrich suffering the same fate as he inflicted on Wright and being driven from office. Censured Representatives are treated like felons and publicly admonished in the well of the House, and the thought of Gingrich experiencing such humiliation was almost too exciting to contemplate. But realists knew that with Gingrich's acknowledgement of wrongdoing, his expressions of regret that 'he brought down on the people's house a controversy which could weaken the faith people have in their government',[39] and the Republican majority standing by their man, the odds against actually bringing Gingrich down were long. But as scandalmongers have long understood, it is sometimes as rewarding to weaken your opponents as to destroy them.

In early 1997, Newt Gingrich was re-elected Speaker of the House of Representatives and, shortly after, he was formally reprimanded by the House and fined $300,000 for violating House rules. The Gingrich

scandal demonstrated the capacity of the majority party to delay proceedings for long periods and to unite around their chosen leader and
protect him from the wrath of their opponents. But what is significant
here is that they were not able to suppress the Gingrich scandals; old
allegations resurfaced and fresh allegations were made. Accusations of
improper conduct against the second most powerful politician in the
country are bound to create newspaper headlines and, while at one level,
Gingrich has survived the storm of scandal, it is not yet clear at what
cost. To some Democrats, it was a good idea to keep Gingrich in office
because the ethics committee is continuing its investigations into other
aspects of Gingrich's alleged misconduct, and his scandals will still be
an issue during the 1998 elections. Getting rid of Gingrich would have
risked seeing him replaced by someone even more aggressive and conservative such as House Majority Leader, Dick Armey, who 'makes
Newt Gingrich look like Mother Teresa'.[40]

The Gingrich scandal is therefore characterized by mixed and conflicting motives. It proved to be long-running and, because of unresolved
allegations, it has still not yet run its course. Nine Republican congressmen declined to vote for Gingrich as Speaker and many others saw the
vote as an opportunity to get Gingrich's attention and co-operation. At
the very least, it seems that Gingrich's authority in the 105th Congress
will be greatly diminished compared to his role in the 104th. Congressional scandals also incur penalties other than institutional discipline,
criminal charges and electoral defeat. A poll in February 1997 suggested
that 60 per cent believed he should resign as Speaker, and his unpopu-
larity scores are even higher. His problem, as Richard Cohen observes,
is that 'few members of Congress have been known to ignore public
opinion polls'.[41]

Conclusion

This analysis of major congressional scandals illustrates the ways in
which these scandals differ from one another and the ways in which,
taken collectively, they differ from the presidential scandals discussed
elsewhere in this book. Yet, while congressional scandals are different
in their origins, character and consequences from presidential scandals,
they are also intimately connected to them in that they share the same
political context and framework.

There are striking differences between congressional scandals in terms
of how they arise, how they develop and how they are resolved. This

chapter has already distinguished between collective and individual scandals but further distinctions can be drawn. Some congressional scandals have their origins in the work of external agencies or externally inspired investigations. Sometimes these agencies, such as the Department of Justice and the FBI, are wholly outside Congress, and sometimes they form part of the legislative support and monitoring structures, for example, the General Accounting Office and its role in the House Banks. Conversely, other scandals are largely generated by attacks by one or more members of Congress on other members, usually of the opposing party.

Scandals therefore arise in some cases out of the normal investigative activities of law-enforcement agencies and sometimes as part of an internal political strategy pursued by members of Congress. External, criminal investigations have distinctive structures and processes, and there is little that members of Congress can do to expedite or prolong such inquiries. But the internal generation of scandal within Congress has created a whole new set of congressional games and strategies designed by the scandalmongers to harass their political opponents. Procedural rules and conventions have become a battleground between those wishing to pile misery on misery and those wanting to cut their losses. The congressional rules and processes for considering allegations of unethical conduct have been abused by both parties and no longer command respect inside or outside Congress.[42] The situation has become so acute that all sides agree on the urgent need for reform. In February 1997, 'House Republican and Democratic leaders have placed a moratorium on the filing of new ethics complaints while they review the chamber's procedures for dealing with members accused of breaking the rules'.[43]

One of the most striking changes which has occurred in the past thirty years is the extent to which the threshold of scandal has fallen. The egregious abuse of privileges and the wholesale acceptance of gifts and money from lobbyists which was quite common in the years before Watergate, seemed to attract little or no public attention, let alone disapproval or punishment. Public and media interest and expectations have now risen dramatically, and members of Congress have to demonstrate that they meet a high standard of public conduct. The charges made against Newt Gingrich pale into insignificance compared to the activities of Congressman Adam Clayton Powell and Senator Thomas Dodd in the 1960s. Many of the allegations made against these men were much more serious than anything Gingrich has faced and, although Powell and Dodd were both disciplined, many serious charges were not even considered by the ethics committees. There is some truth in the judgement of one conservative on the Newt Gingrich case, 'for two years the left has lived in hope of a "smoking gun" and it comes up with a parking ticket'.[44]

Clearly, the consequences of scandal have varied enormously for members depending on the gravity and nature of the offences, the status and popularity of the members concerned, the partizan balance in Congress, the style and strength of the defence and the presence or likelihood of criminal charges. Thus, we find that what look like similar examples of improper conduct attract different penalties. It may be argued that, over time, attitudes and standards evolve so that it is wrong to judge 1990s scandals by 1970s standards, but the cases of Alan Cranston, one of the Keating Five, and Speaker Jim Wright stand interesting comparison. Whereas Cranston, alone of the Keating Five, was singled out for reprimand by the Senate because of his interventions on behalf of a Savings and Loan operator, Jim Wright's even more egregious intervention in the same field were dismissed by the House Committee as merely 'intemperate'. Standards have certainly changed over the decades and, what was once normal behaviour in Congress is now regarded as scandalous, but the Cranston and Wright cases were only two years apart. It seems that the way Congress deals with scandal has not only changed but has also become more inconsistent and unpredictable.

Scandals of a certain sort seem to provoke the severest congressional response. Bribery in its most simple and unambiguous form tends to attract the harshest treatment while 'intemperate' constituency service is often condoned or only mildly rebuked. But the stuff of congressional scandal lies in the need to raise campaign finance and the reciprocities that implies. Congress has expressed its determination to reform its own ethics procedures but does not seem to have any clear idea of how to do it, and the same can be said of campaign-finance reform. One of the many ironies of congressional scandal is that it is not always easy to distinguish the scandalous from the honest reformer. A campaign finance bill was introduced in early 1997 and its cosponsor was Senator John McCain (R-Arizona) of Keating Five fame who believes that some congressional campaign practices are illegal. McCain's reformist approach has caused some nervousness among his Republican colleagues who are keen to use campaign finance as a scandal issue to condemn the irregularities in the Democrats' Presidential fund-raising in 1996. Once again, the problem is that, once scandal issues are raised, they can be turned back against the accusers.

In looking at congressional and presidential scandals, there are clear differences in the kind of improper behaviour under scrutiny, the mechanisms and control of investigations, the intensity of media coverage and the consequent impact on public opinion. According to some polls, most Americans believe that Newt Gingrich is dishonest, untrustworthy and a law-breaker [45] but relatively few have a clear idea of what he is supposed to have done. The actions and misdeeds of presidents are more widely publicized and the misconduct of Nixon in Watergate and Reagan in Iran–Contra are widely understood.

Congressional scandals do not seem to emanate from policy differences with presidents but presidential scandals regularly derive from inter-institutional conflicts over the power of the presidency. Executive privilege, the direction of foreign policy, presidential findings, the withholding of intelligence information and the refusal to respond to congressional subpoenas have featured in different degrees in the major presidential scandals of modern times. Members of Congress regularly pressurize the attorney-general to ask the Court of Appeal to appoint independent counsel to investigate scandals in the executive branch, but Congress decides for itself when to investigate itself and who should do it. Whereas independent counsels are sometimes thought to be out of control – for example, Walsh's seven-year investigation of Iran–Contra – congressional special counsels seem to be under closer control, for example, the direction and timing of Cole's investigation of Gingrich.

If congressional scandals sometimes involve the abuse of office, they rarely involve the abuse of power. In presidential scandals, the emphasis is on the illegitimate use of presidential power at home or overseas. In comparison, congressional scandals often seem trivial and petty involving, as they do, relatively small sums of money and the abuse of minor privileges. Members of Congress do not initiate secret wars, trade with terrorists and drug dealers, organize burglaries and domestic surveillance operations or conspire to conceal their involvement in illegal activities. Not only do presidential scandals seem more substantial, in that the president can wield the power of the federal government to pursue his policy ends, but they normally have an additional dimension, in that as much, if not more, scandal is generated by attempts to conceal the substantive scandal.

If presidential scandals are frequently associated with the ideas of deception, 'cover-up' and 'damage-limitation strategies', congressional scandals seem to lack these vital elements. Where legislators believe that one of their own has tried to deceive Congress, as in the case of Senator Packwood and his diaries, the response is unforgiving. But members of Congress lack the organizational resources and authority to initiate a cover-up and, normally, the character of congressional scandals does not justify the effort.

What is clear is that Congress has not escaped the heightened public concerns and expectations generated by Watergate, Iran–Contra and other executive-branch scandals. Congress reserves the right to discipline its own members for improper conduct and this tends to encourage the media to question the fairness, independence and accountability of the process. Corruption and misconduct are easy to allege but difficult to prove or disprove, and it is little wonder that members of Congress compete to avoid serving on the Senate and House ethics committees.

Legislators believe that scandals are whipped up by the media and they regard the media as cynical, negative, unfair and biased. The press and television obviously have a large role in determining what is a scandal, how much attention to give it and for how long. Some observers and, no doubt, many members of Congress believe that the public distrust and scandal-ridden image of Congress can be attributed to its intensely negative press coverage.[46]

But while the media's role is clearly important, legislators have themselves greatly contributed to their current image. Partizanship has been taken to new heights, and the 1996 congressional elections give further confirmation that candidates trailing in the polls frequently go negative, and a cycle of escalating attacks is set in train. It is not just that character-assassination, negative campaigning and scandals have become the normal mode of congressional politics but that no one knows how to stop or where to draw the line. If the media are negative about Congress, and members of Congress are negative about one another, where does that leave the public in their evaluations of scandals in Congress? The current public perception, which seems unlikely to change in the near future, is that where there is smoke there is fire, and where there is scandal there are guilty members of Congress, and where there are no convictions or punishment, there is a cover-up. The interaction of public distrust, media cynicism and congressional panic accounts for the periodic outbreaks of 'mindless cannibalism'[47] in Congress and the perpetuation of its image as a scandal-ridden institution.

Notes

1. The Baker, Powell and Dodd scandals are discussed, in very different ways, in Robert S. Getz, *Congressional Ethics* (Princeton: Van Nostrand Company, 1966) and Drew Pearson and Jack Anderson, *The Case Against Congress* (New York: Simon and Schuster, 1968).

2. The formal title is *Ethics Manual for Members, Offices and Employees of the U.S. House of Representatives*, the Committee on Standards of Official Conduct, 102nd Congress, 2nd Session (U.S. Government Printing Office 53–007, Washington, April 1992).

3. Robin Moore, *The Washington Connection* (New York, London, 1977), pp. 1–74.

4. This prompted a number of Congressional investigations but see also *Congressional Ethics: History, Facts, and Controversy* (Washington: Congressional Quarterly, 1992), pp. 63–8.

5. Stephen Pizzo et al., *Inside Job: The Looting of America's Savings and Loan* (New York: McGraw Hill, 1989), pp. 263–97; Dennis F. Thompson, 'Mediated Corruption: The Case of the Keating Five', *American Political Science Review*, vol. 87, No. 2, June 1993, pp. 369–81.

6. Gary C. Jacobson and Michael A. Dimock, 'Checking Out: The Effects of Bank Overdrafts on the 1992 Elections', *American Journal of Political Science*, vol. 38, August 1994, pp. 601–24; Charles Stewart III, 'Let's go fly a kite: Correlates of Involvement in the House Bank Scandal', *Legislative Studies Quarterly*, vol. XIX, No. 4, 1994, pp. 521–36.

7. Dennis F. Thompson, *Ethics in Congress: From Individual to Institutional Corruption* (Washington D.C.: The Brookings Institution, 1995), p. 1.

8. Steven V. Roberts, 'Senators and Senate on Trial with Williams', *New York Times*, 10 March 1982, p. B2.

9. Thompson, 1995, p. 104. See also, *In the Matter of John W. Jenrette Jr*, Committee Print, House Committee on Standards of Official Conduct, 96 Cong. 2 Sess. (Government Printing Office, December 1980).

10. Thompson, 1995, p. 105. See also 'Senator Williams's Innocent Intentions', *Investigations of Senator Harrison A. Williams Jr.. Response of Senator Williams*, Committee Print, Senate Select Committee on Ethics, 97 Cong. 1 Sess. (Government Printing Office, September, 1981), p. 5.

11. D. H. Lowenstein, 'Political Bribery and the Intermediate Theory of Politics', *UCLA Law Review*, 32, 1985, pp. 796–8; James Lindgren, 'The Elusive Distinction between Bribery and Extortion', *UCLA Law Review*, 35, 1988, pp. 819–909.

12. Thompson, 1995, p. 220.

13. Henry N. Pontell and Kitty Calavita, 'White Collar Crime in the Savings and Loan Scandal', *The Annals*, January 1993, p. 32. See also James Ring Adams, *The Big Fix: Inside the S. and L. Scandal* (New York: John Wiley, 1990).

14. Thompson, 1993, p. 370.

15. Pontell and Calavita, p. 39.

16. Thompson, 1993, p. 379.

17. Thompson, 1993, p. 141. See also *Investigation of Senator Alan Cranston together with*

Additional Views, Committee Print, Senate Select Committee on Ethics, 102 Cong. 2 Sess. (Government Printing Office, November 1991).

18. Thompson, 1993, p. 374.
19. Cranston was not alone in wondering why he had been singled out. See Jill Abramson and David Rogers 'The Keating 535: Five Are on the Grill but Other Lawmakers Help Big Donors Too', *Wall Street Journal*, 10 January 1991, pp. A1, A6; and Amitai Etzioni, 'Keating Six?', *Responsive Community*, vol. 1, Winter, 1990–91, pp. 6–9.
20. Suzanne Garment, *Scandal: The Crisis of Mistrust in American Politics* (New York: Times Books, Random House, 1991), p. 248.
21. Susan A. Banducci and Jeffrey A. Karp, 'Electoral Consequences of Scandal and Reapportionment in the 1992 House Elections', *American Politics Quarterly*, vol. 22, January 1994, pp. 3–26; Jacobson and Dimock, 1994.
22. Thompson, 1995, p. 62.
23. Stewart III, p. 532.
24. CBS/*New York Times* survey, 26–29 March 1992, Roper Center for Public Opinion Research, University of Connecticut.
25. Stewart III, p. 521
26. Thompson, 1995, pp. 62–3.
27. *In the Matter of Representative James C. Wright Jr.*, Committee Print, House Committee on Standards of Official Conduct, 101 Cong. 2 Sess. (Government Printing Office, April 1989): John M. Barry, *The Ambition and the Power* (New York: Viking, 1989); see also the discussion in Thompson, 1995, pp. 43–8.
28. The Gingrich scandals are on-going and, as yet, there is a paucity of academic analyses. There is a wealth of internet and newspaper coverage: see especially the *Washington Post* in the period 19.12.96–22.2.97.; Richard Lacayo, 'House Squeaker', *Time*, 13 January 1997, pp. 20–4; *Statement of Alleged Violation in the Matter of Representative Newt Gingrich*, House Committee on Standards of Official Conduct, 104 Cong. 2 Sess, 21 December 1996.
29. Michael Foley and John E. Owens, *Congress and the Presidency* (Manchester: Manchester University Press, 1996), p. 36.
30. *In the Matter of Wright*, pp. 90–1.
31. Ibid., pp. 83–4.
32. Ibid., p. 63.
33. *Congressional Ethics*, 1992, pp. 106–7.
34. *Houston Chronicle*, 7 December 1995.
35. 'Group Books "Ethics Adviser" to Review Gingrich Book Deal', *Washington Post*, 3 February 1995, p. A14.
36. Robert Williams and Esther Jubb, 'Shutting Down Government: Budget Crises in the American Political System', *Parliamentary Affairs*, vol. 49, No. 3, July 1996, pp. 471–84.
37. *Politics Now: Congress Daily* (internet), 'Gingrich Ethics Committee Cases Flare Up in House', 20 September 1996, p. 1.
38. *Washington Post*, 24 December 1996, p. A01.
39. *Washington Post*, 22 December 1996, p. A01.
40. *Washington Post*, 30 December 1996, p. A01.
41. *National Journal*, 22 February 1997, citing poll in *Los Angeles Times*.
42. J. Dumbrell, 'Corruption and Ethics Codes in Congress', *Corruption and Reform*, vol. 6, No. 2, 1991, pp. 147–70.

43. *National Journal*, 22 February 1997.
44. *Washington Post*, 24 December 1996, p. A01.
45. *ABC News Poll*, 27 January 1997.
46. J. N. Capella and Katherine Hall Jamieson, 'News Frames, Political Cynicism and Media Cynicism', *Annals*, July 1996, pp. 71–84; and Thomas E. Patterson, 'Bad News, Bad Governance', *Annals*, July 1996, pp. 97–108; see also Mark J. Rozell, *In Contempt of Congress: Postwar Press Coverage on Capitol Hill* (New York: Praeger, 1996).
47. Dumbrell, p. 147, quoting Speaker Jim Wright's resignation speech.

CHAPTER 6

The Place of Scandals in American Political Life

Dirty tricks in American elections did not begin with 'tricky Dicky' Nixon, and Ronald Reagan was not the first president to deceive Congress. Jim Wright and Newt Gingrich are not the only congressional politicians to have evaded campaign finance rules, and unsuccessful business ventures are not unique to Bill Clinton. What these politicians have in common is that they were found out and their conduct subjected to intense and extended scrutiny. Their quest for electoral, financial and policy advantage involved actions and judgements which have subsequently been tested in a variety of tribunals, not least in the court of public opinion.

Political scandals are public events in the sense that, through the oxygen of publicity, they expose conduct which would otherwise remain private or be known only to a restricted circle of political insiders. The politicians involved in the scandals discussed in this book behaved as they did in the expectation that knowledge of their conduct would be kept from their electorates, their political opponents and the media. In short, political scandals transform private or secret conduct into public controversy. The public may be suspicious and even cynical about the behaviour of their political leaders but, if they are ignorant of actual misconduct, they can scarcely be scandalized by it.

The origin of every political scandal is some form of revelation or disclosure about the conduct of politicians which hitherto was not in the public domain and which encourages the public to see those identified in a new light. The revelation usually appears in the American press or television by means of internal 'leaks', public-interest-group allegations, official admissions, investigative journalism or the foreign press. In Watergate, junior reporters stumbled on to a story which grew far beyond their usual horizons. In Iran–Contra, *Al-Shiraa*, a Lebanese weekly, blew the whistle on the clandestine overtures to Iran. In the case of Whitewater, the original investigative reporting came from the

New York Times, but subsequent sensational allegations appeared in the British *Sunday Telegraph*. Partizan rivalry has ensured that, since the 1980s, the American media's attention has been focused on scandal allegations involving members of Congress.

Mainstream media reports of scandal are not usually conjured out of thin air. Their origins are real events: the Watergate burglary; the shooting down of a CIA plane in Nicaragua; McFarlane's visit to Tehran; Clinton's partnership with Jim McDougal; and the activities of charitable foundations linked to Newt Gingrich. The revelations themselves do not always generate immediate scandals but, more often, trigger a series of questions about the conduct of politicians. An unwillingness or inability to answer such questions excites further media interest and generates more questions. A continuing or perceived inability to provide comprehensive and persuasive answers gives rise to demands for one or more forms of official inquiry to find the real answers to unresolved issues.

Watergate has provided a model and a yardstick for later scandals but, in some ways, this is misleading. Watergate was a 'slow-burn' kind of scandal in which the proportions and seriousness of the scandal only gradually became apparent. In its first phase, it was ignored by much of the mass media whose investigative appetites and capacity are frequently much exaggerated. The media more often respond to the work of other institutions than undertake any serious or sustained inquiries themselves. While scandals may sell newspapers and boost ratings, digging for dirt is an expensive and time-consuming activity and usually undertaken only when there is other strong evidence pointing to the existence and location of a mother lode of scandal. Students of American politics whose knowledge of Watergate is primarily derived from the movie, *All The President's Men*, tend to be convinced that Redford and Hoffman (a.k.a. Woodward and Bernstein) were solely responsible for discovering the misconduct, tracing it up through the White House and the CRP, and ultimately forcing the resignation of President Nixon. The reality is more complex and the achievements of the Pulitzer Prize-winning journalists more modest than Hollywood would have us believe. But whether the media are parasitic upon the revelations of others or not, their role is crucial both in broadening and deepening public interest and in accelerating the political momentum which carries a particular scandal forward.

Irrespective of the mechanism of revelation, the next important phase is the extent and form of political, public and media reaction. The judgements made by editorial writers, news anchors, interest groups and the wider political community all have their impact on public opinion and the extent to which it is mobilized in support of or opposition to the politicians at the centre of the scandal. The revelations themselves and the political heat they generate in turn help to shape the response of law-enforcement agencies and officials, the attorney-general and congressional committees.

The reaction to scandal revelations is dictated by the political context and climate in which they occur. The stage of the electoral cycle, the partizan balance in Congress, the president's approval ratings and electoral mandate, all play a part in influencing the form, speed and tone of the reaction. The odds on successful prosecution, the likelihood of congressional hearings and the political, financial and administrative consequences of the scandal all need to be assessed.

Since Watergate, a key question in presidential and other executive-branch scandals is how best to conduct an independent investigation which avoids conflicts of interest. The initial answer was for the Justice department to appoint a prosecutor from outside the ranks of the department. But the 'Saturday Night Massacre' and the dismissal of Special Prosecutor, Archibald Cox, suggested that the independence of the prosecutor needed to be further protected by establishing a different procedure for appointment and a higher threshold for removal. The Ethics in Government Act of 1978 created the institution of the more neutral-sounding independent counsel, and it is this relatively new office which was responsible for the extended investigation of Iran–Contra and which is conducting lengthy inquiries into Whitewater and related scandals.

The history of special prosecutors and independent counsels in American political scandals has not been a happy one. The appointment, conduct and accountability of independent counsels have now become part of the culture of scandal. The controversies deriving from Walsh's interminable investigations of Iran–Contra and the political cloud surrounding the appointment of Starr to investigate Whitewater have thrust the role and powers of independent counsels into the heart of contemporary debates about political scandal in the United States. Once the autonomy of the independent counsel was established, attention was bound to be centred on the politics of the appointment process and the ambitions and motivations of the particular independent counsel chosen.

It has proved easier to establish the legal and institutional independence of the office of independent counsel than it has to develop support for the view that independent counsels are immune from partizan loyalties and ambitions.

As the tide of political scandal rises, waves of demands to appoint an independent counsel flood the office of the attorney-general. If the attorney-general refuses to appoint an independent counsel, the integrity of the attorney-general will be called into question. There have been attorney-generals in the past, including, Robert Kennedy, John Mitchell and Ed Meese, who were personally close to their presidents and whose independence and objectivity in making quasi-judicial decisions likely to threaten their political masters could be questioned. But, in practice, Meese's closeness to Reagan was so well known that it made it difficult for Meese to refuse demands for independent counsels without appearing to compromise his integrity. Sleaze allegations against members of the Reagan administration were so plentiful that Meese found himself appointing independent counsels even when the alleged misconduct was relatively trivial. Uniquely, Meese twice found himself the subject of independent counsel investigations.

Recent scandals have highlighted a number of problems, most obviously distinguishing between whales and minnows and discriminating between the political clout of the accusers and the weight of the actual evidence. The office of independent counsel was created in the wake of Watergate, the most important scandal in American political history, but it has been used subsequently in cases of much less significance. When the demand for the appointment comes from Congress, the attorney-general is required to explain to Congress if it is decided to take no action. When the legislature and executive are under divided control, the political pressures on the attorney-general are considerable.

In the 1980s, Republicans accused Democrats of using the independent-counsel machinery to undermine the Reagan administration and, in the 1990s, the Democrats made the same charge against Republicans with regard to the investigation of Whitewater and associated scandals. Partizanship and institutional rivalry bedevil the office of independent counsel and, while many in both parties agree on the need for reform of the office, it is too valuable a weapon in the scandal wars to expect early agreement. In the criminal justice system, prosecutors prosecute when they think they have enough evidence to convict but, in the world of independent counsels, reports are sometimes written which cast doubt on the ethics of public officials but stop short of recommending prosecution. Public officials targeted by independent counsels are put to great personal cost and are often forced to resign their offices to defend themselves. An independent counsel investigation is now a defining characteristic of a political scandal and, even when prosecutions do not follow, the reputations and careers of those investigated are often badly damaged.

In April 1997, Attorney-General Janet Reno came under severe attack from Republican leaders for not immediately acceding to their demands that she appoint an independent counsel to investigate Democrat fundraising in the 1996 presidential election. Newt Gingrich has compared Reno to Richard Nixon's attorney-general 'the feloniously dishonest' [1] John Mitchell. Reno is not a FOB (friend of Bill) and is by no means a Clinton insider, but such attacks give one measure of the pressures exerted by the majority in Congress in their efforts to institutionalize what they hope will be a major political scandal for the Democrat Party.

The reaction to Watergate produced a significant institutional reform, the office of independent counsel. But this office investigates wrongdoing only in the executive branch. While Congress has frequently displayed enthusiasm for the appointment of such counsels to investigate the president and his staff, it has shown a contrasting reluctance to allow such independent investigators loose in Congress. When it comes to the alleged transgressions of its own members, Congress prefers to keep control of its own investigation processes. It does increasingly use special counsels to assist the two ethics committees but there is no question of handing over the appointing power to the judiciary.

Congress has a clear preference for executive-branch scandal and, while routine congressional oversight of the executive branch is generally thought tedious, the whiff of presidential scandal in the years since Watergate has attracted serious congressional attention. In the 1970s there were congressional demands for inquiries into the activities of President Carter's brother, his chief-of-staff and his Director of OMB. In the 1980s, in addition to Iran–Contra, there were demands for investigations of Reagan's national security adviser, members of the White House staff and several cabinet members.

While the White House's ability to manage a presidential scandal is profoundly weakened by the appointment of an independent counsel, Congress can take centre stage in scandal resolution by holding its own hearings and conducting its own investigations of any matter it chooses.

But, just as the threshold for scandal investigation seems to have been progressively lowered, so the impact of congressional hearings seems to have diminished over time. In a sense, the Watergate hearings set a standard that it has proved impossible to match. The Iran–Contra hearings had their elements of drama and commanded public attention but they did not convince anyone that the members of the joint congressional committee were national heroes engaged in productive inquiries. Whereas Watergate was a 'slow-burn' scandal, in which the story emerged piece by piece thus adding to the drama and tension, Iran–Contra was a 'flame-out' in which almost all the vital information became public within a short period of time. The two sets of Whitewater hearings have set new lows in congressional inquiries in that both have been transparently partisan and unable to persuade a sceptical public that their interests were being protected or advanced. To hunters of scandal, 'smoking guns' excite interest but meandering 'fishing expeditions' seem petty and pointless. In this respect, Whitewater may prove to be less of a 'slow burn' and more of a damp squib.

One significant feature of the reactions to scandal revelations is how little they produce in the way of political reforms. Watergate is an exception here but its major institutional legacy, the independent counsel, has itself attracted much criticism. The behaviour of Walsh in Iran–Contra infuriated Republicans, and Starr's conduct in Whitewater has distressed Democrats. Scandals tend to be explained largely in terms of errors of judgement, excessive zeal, lack of supervision, personality clashes and rivalries, and the individual culpability of members of the presidential staff. Watergate is the exception to the congressional rule that constitutional confrontation with the presidency is normally best avoided. The 'invitation to struggle' over foreign policy, graphically illustrated in Iran–Contra, continues unresolved. The Watergate impeachment articles relating to presidential power were defeated and the relative roles of the president and Congress were reduced to platitudes in the congressional reports on Iran–Contra.

It seems that, where presidential scandal is concerned, Congress is content to play a quasi-judicial role. The scandal is defined in terms of specific, preferably illegal, conduct by particular individuals. In this way, inter-institutional political and policy conflicts are transformed into legal and judicial debates about the conduct of individuals. As the prospect of impeachment recedes, so the scandal diminishes. When prosecutions are brought and trials conducted, the scandal grows again. In the case of Iran–Contra, the Reagan administration was able to defuse the scandal further by withholding, allegedly on national security grounds, crucial information which allowed North and Poindexter to appeal successfully against their convictions. Ultimately, presidents can protect those who have helped them by exercising the power of pardon, as Ford did for Nixon, as Bush did for Weinberger and as Clinton might yet do for Susan McDougal.

The separated character of the American political system[2] means that scandals evolve in a fragmented and staccato way. The Justice Department may investigate allegations and then find that at least some of its work is usurped by the appointment of an independent counsel. Congressional hearings sometimes co-operate and sometimes compete with independent-counsel investigations. The emerging scandal surfaces from time to time in different parts of the political system. The different players, the president and his staff, members of Congress, prosecutors, judges, witnesses and scoop-hungry journalists all stir the scandal pot. The result is an untidy mess. It is not possible to give an account of a major political scandal in the form of a single, unbroken narrative. There is always something else going on outside the main narrative. There seems almost to be a competition between the media, the White House, the Congress, independent counsels and the courts for ownership and control of scandals. Each party's claim is partial and no institution is able to co-ordinate the different elements, let alone control the entire scandal process. The result is that, instead of a single, unbroken narrative, we face disconnected, fragmented, overlapping, multiple narratives. Political scandals are rarely neat, tidy affairs which fit conveniently into clearly labelled institutional and procedural boxes.

But if scandals resist orchestration and central direction, there are two recent developments in American politics which seem to bear some responsibility for the increased incidence of political scandals: the changed role of the mass media and the use of scandal allegations as a first-strike weapon. Political scandals are manifestations of negativity[3] in American politics exemplified both by negative media coverage of politics and political institutions and by the negative attacks of politicians on one another. The transformation of the media from poodles to watchdogs to Rottweilers has undoubtedly contributed to the increasing prominence and importance of political scandals. If policy details and differences are complex and boring to readers, allegations of personal wrongdoing are simpler to report and likely to be more interesting to more readers.

In Larry Sabato's memorable phrase, 'the news media, print and broadcast, go after a wounded politician like sharks in a feeding frenzy'.[4] While this may be a lurid overstatement, Sabato makes the more important point that, in focusing on scandal, 'journalists now take centre stage in the process, creating the news as much as reporting it'.[5] President Clinton acceded to demands to appoint an independent counsel for Whitewater partly because journalists at home and abroad would not allow him to address any other domestic or foreign issues. News conferences and meetings with foreign heads of state were disrupted by choruses of questions about Whitewater and helped disrupt the president's own agenda. Recent studies have argued that the way the mass media cover politics has made a major contribution to encouraging a cynical and passive view of public life.[6] The idealistic views of government and politics found in Almond and Verba's famous 1960s study of political culture have long since disappeared.[7] In the 1990s, the majority distrusts government and tends to see politicians as corrupt and self-serving.

The mass media have clearly had a role in shaping public attitudes toward government and politicians. Americans no longer regard their presidents as a combination of Daniel Boone and Jesus Christ. In the 1950s, President Eisenhower may have physically resembled every American child's image of God but, in the 1990s, President Clinton is more often depicted in the conservative press as the devil incarnate. Richard Nixon is usually blamed for this transformation of public attitudes but the decline in trust began before Watergate. While it is easy to condemn contemporary cynicism and its corroding influence on American politics, it can scarcely be argued that a vigorous democracy requires its press to conceal the blemishes and faults of its leaders or that its citizens should accept on faith what their leaders choose to tell them.

Before the mass media are condemned for distorting the political agenda with their overemphasis on scandal, it is appropriate to consider to what extent the American political classes are the architects of their own misfortune. If people do not trust politicians, is it because the newspapers have told them that politicians are all liars and crooks? Or is it that modern political experience suggests that politicians promise more than they deliver and that they frequently exploit their public positions for partizan or private advantage? It is the disjunctions which seem to offend public sensibilities, the disjunctions between preaching family values and being sexually promiscuous, between swearing to implement the law while finding ways to evade or obstruct it, and between the commitment to public service and the practice of personal enrichment. While politicians regard the media as cynical, confrontational, intrusive, biased and unfair, the public inclines to the view that a vigilant, sceptical media is the best hope of keeping politicians honest.

If sober realism about politicians and government is preferable to misplaced idealism, the behaviour of politicians toward one another has made its distinctive contribution to generating scandals and eroding public confidence in the integrity of the political process. In the 1980s and 1990s, partizanship has been taken to new heights and bipartizanship in Congress and elsewhere looks increasingly unnatural. Recent elections offered further confirmation that 'going negative' is fashionable and successful as a campaign tactic. Negative-campaign conduct has permeated the legislative process and has disrupted the traditional norms of congressional life.

It sometimes seems as if partizanship has reached the status of a vendetta, a blood feud, when every criticism or attack on a member of one faction has to be met with an equally strong counterattack. In the 1980s, congressional Republicans not only believed that their Democrat colleagues were grossly exaggerating the amount of sleaze in the Reagan administration,[8] but they also believed that long-standing control of the House of Representatives allowed the Democratic leadership to treat Republicans with contempt. The well-known campaign against Speaker Jim Wright, orchestrated by Newt Gingrich, was the most conspicuous example of political payback. The Republican congressional triumph in 1994 and Gingrich's elevation to the speakership almost guaranteed that Democrats would seek revenge.

The problem is not just that 'character attacks, negative campaigning and scandals have become the normal mode of politics'[9] but rather that no one knows how to stop or where to draw the line. In the nuclear arms race, neither side would give way until the Soviets could no longer afford the weapons and ammunition. But neither side seems short of ammunition in the American war of scandal and neither side has any political incentive to lay down its weapons.

Political scandal has sometimes been dismissed as a superficial feature of American politics, a sordid, if sometimes fascinating, distraction from the real business of politics and government. But to dismiss political scandal as the froth on the political cappuccino is to avoid answering a central question: what drives American politics? What shapes and guides the behaviour of American politicians? There are, of course, institutional structures and procedures but they are, in an important sense, neutral in that they can be operated in a variety of ways. What principles guide the operation of this machinery?

Students of American politics have long appreciated that political ideology is not a conspicuous feature of American political life. In 1996, the ideologies of the main presidential candidates, a new Democrat and an old Republican, were virtually indistinguishable. It has sometimes been argued that the real conflicts in American politics are not at the level of ideology but involve specific policies and programmes, different means to shared goals. This argument looks a little shaky in the 1990s. It has always rested on the doubtful assumptions that policy issues and debates resonate with voters and that they can discriminate between the different positions of candidates and parties. But the policy differences between the parties have blurred further since the election of Clinton. His willingness, particularly since 1994, to embrace traditional Republican policies on issues such as welfare make it difficult to identify significant policy differences. Political ideology and policy debates are therefore not useful guides to the battleground of American politics. To an unprecedented extent, political scandals now serve as the battleground for contending political forces.

It looks increasingly as if political scandals have evolved in ways likely to revive the fortunes of that long-derided American political dinosaur, the political party. The decline of parties in American elections and politics has been exhaustively documented.[10] Students of American politics know that elections have become increasingly candidate-centred and that central party organizations lack the control over candidates and policies enjoyed by many of their European counterparts. But political scandals now seem to offer an important means of bringing individuals and parties together for political purposes.

If there is little point in trying to evaluate politics and politicians in terms of ideologies, programmes and policies, there may be some point in assessing their characters. In a fragmented, separated system, no aspiring president can guarantee to deliver on his promises, but voters can make judgements about their seriousness of purpose, their personal principles and their political values. Political scandals offer an obvious and convenient way to assess character in the broadest sense. Political scandals deal with lies, deception, cover-up, the obstruction of justice and contempt for political opponents, and legitimate political processes and standards. The electoral success of the Republicans in the 1994 congressional elections was partly due to the image of their opponents generated by the House Banking scandal. More Democrats than Republicans had run up overdrafts and the Democrat overdrafts were larger than the Republican overdrafts. These individual overdrafts were spun together to make a political scandal which suggested that long-standing Democrat control of the House had bred an arrogance of power and a belief that the majority could do whatever they wanted without fear of electoral retribution. The earlier attacks on Speaker Jim Wright also helped to give the minority Republicans a common purpose and, in the same way, the subsequent attacks on Speaker Newt Gingrich helped unify the minority Democrats after the 1994 election.

This book rejects the view that political scandals are superficial epiphenomena and suggests that they have assumed a central place in the contemporary American political process. In a period when ideological and policy consensus has broken out, political scandals help the electorate to differentiate between politicians and parties. For politicians, the scandal wars help to unify party organizations which would otherwise lack cohesion. In 1996, congressional Republicans rallied to support their beleaguered leader, Newt Gingrich, and re-elected him Speaker of the House of Representatives. Similarly, congressional Democrats have united to oppose Republican attempts to exploit the Whitewater scandal against President Clinton. Not all scandals are equal, and some are obviously more equal than others. The re-election of President Clinton seems to support the view that the electorate can distinguish a Whitewater from a Watergate. It seems incontrovertible that political scandals have now acquired a prominent and important place in American political life and there are no signs that their political significance is likely to diminish.

Notes

1. Richard Cohen, 'Judging by Janet Reno's Critics', *Washington Post*, 17 April 1997, p. A23.
2. The nature of this system and the presidency's place in it is most clearly explained in Charles O. Jones, *The Presidency in a Separated System* (Washington: Brookings Institution, 1994).
3. Stephen Ansolabehere and Shanto Iyengar, *Going Negative: How Political*

Advertisements Shrink and Polarize the Electorate (New York: The Free Press, 1993), p. 1.

4. Larry J. Sabato, *Feeding Frenzy: How Attack Journalism Has Transformed American Politics* (New York: The Free Press, 1993), p. 1.

5. Ibid., p. 1.

6. James Fallows, *Breaking the News: How the Media Undermine American Democracy* (New York: Pantheon, 1996).

7. Gabriel A. Almond and Sidney Verba, *The Civic Culture: Political Attitudes and Democracy in Five Nations* (Princeton, NJ: Princeton University Press, 1963).

8. For a discussion of sleaze in the Reagan administration, see Robert Williams, 'Private Interests and Public Office: The American Experience of Sleaze', *Parliamentary Affairs*, vol. 48, No. 4, 1995, pp. 641–2.

9. William Schneider, *National Journal*, 21 May 1994, p. 1218.

10. Martin P. Wattenberg, *The Decline of American Political Parties, 1952–1988* (Cambridge, Mass.: Harvard University Press, 1988).

Select Bibliography

General

Barker, Anthony, 'The Upturned Stone: Political Scandals in Twenty Democracies and their Investigation Processes', *Essex Papers in Politics and Government*, No. 90, 1992.

Corruption and Reform, special issue on political scandal, vol. 3, No. 3, 1988–9.

Garment, Suzanne, *Scandal: the Crisis of Mistrust in American Politics* (New York: Times Books, Random House, 1991).

King, Anthony, 'Sex, Money and Power: Political Scandals in Great Britain and the United States', *Essex Papers in Politics and Government*, No. 14, 1984.

Kohn, George C., *Encyclopaedia of American Scandal* (New York: Facts on File, 1989).

Longman, *Political Scandals and Causes Célèbres since 1945: an International Reference Compendium* (Harlow: Longman, 1991).

Markovits, A. S. and Silverstein, M., *The Politics of Scandal: Power and Process in Liberal Democracies* (New York: Holmes and Meier, 1988).

Williams, Robert, 'Private Interests and Public Office: The American Experience of Sleaze', *Parliamentary Affairs*, vol. 48, No. 4, 1995, pp. 632–49.

Watergate

Ben-Veniste, Richard and Frampton, George Jr, *Stonewall: The Real Story of The Watergate Prosecution* (New York: Simon and Schuster, 1977).

Bernstein, Carl and Woodward, Bob, *All The President's Men* (New York: Simon and Schuster, 1974).

Congressional Quarterly Inc., *Watergate: Chronology of a Crisis*, Wayne Kelley (exec. ed.), Washington D.C., 1975.

Dean, John W. II, *Blind Ambition: The White House Years* (New York: Simon and Schuster, 1976).

Emery, Fred, *Watergate: The Corruption and Fall of Richard M. Nixon* (London: Jonathan Cape, 1994).

Haldeman, H. R., *The Ends of Power* (New York: Times Books, 1978).

Hougan, Jim, *Secret Agenda: Watergate, Deep Throat and the CIA* (New York: Random House, 1984).

Jaworski, Leon, *The Right and the Power: The Prosecution of Watergate* (New York: Reader's Digest, 1976).

Kutler, Stanley I., *The Wars of Watergate: The Last Crisis of Richard Nixon* (New York: Knopf, 1990).

LaRue, L. H., *Political Discourse: A Case Study of the Watergate Affair* (Athens and London: University of Georgia Press, 1988).

Liddy, G. Gordon, *Will* (New York: St Martin's Press, 1980).

Lukas, Anthony J., *Nightmare: The Underside of the Nixon Years* (New York: Viking, 1976).

Magruder, Jeb Stuart, *An American Life* (New York: Atheneum, 1974).

Nixon, Richard M., *RN: The Memoirs of Richard Nixon* (New York: Grosset and Dunlap, 1975).

Schudson, Michael, *Watergate in American Memory* (New York: Basic Books, 1992).

Sirica, John, *To Set the Record Straight: The Break-in, the Tapes, the Conspirators, the Pardon* (New York: Norton, 1979).

White, Theodore H., *Breach of Faith: The Fall of Richard Nixon* (New York: Atheneum, 1975).

Iran–Contra

Congressional Quarterly, *The Iran–Contra Puzzle* (Washington, 1987).

Cornfield, M. and Yalof, David Alistair, 'Innocent by reason of analogy: How the Watergate analogy served both Reagan and the press during the Iran–Contra affair', *Corruption and Reform*, vol. 3, No. 2, 1988–89, pp. 185–206.

Draper, Theodore, 'The Rise of the American Junta', *New York Review of Books*, 8 October 1987.

Draper, Theodore, *A Very Thin Line: The Iran–Contra Affair* (New York: Hill and Wang, 1991).

Foley, Michael, *Mumbling Across the Branches: The Iran–Contra Scandal, the Boland Amendments, and the American Foreign Policy Making Process*, Aberystwyth: International Politics Research Papers, No. 6.

Kornbluh, Peter and Byrne, Malcolm (eds), *The Iran–Contra Scandal: The Declassified History* (New York: The New Press, 1993).

McFarlane, Robert C. with Zofia Smardz, *Special Trust* (New York: Cadell and Davies, 1994).

Schraeder, Peter J., *Intervention in the 1980s: US Foreign Policy in the Third World* (Boulder: Lynne Rienner Publishers, 1989).

U.S. Congress *Report of the Congressional Committee Investigating the Iran–Contra Affair* (Washington D.C.: Government Printing Office, 1987).

Walsh, Lawrence E., *Iran–Contra: The Final Report* (New York: Times Books, 1994).

Williams, Robert, 'Presidential power and the abuse of office: The case of the Iran–Contra affair', *Corruption and Reform*, vol. 3, No. 2, 1988, pp. 171–83.

Williams, Robert, 'The last word on the Iran–Contra Affair?', *Crime, Law and Social Change*, vol. 23, 1995, pp. 367–85.

Woodward, Bob, *Veil: The Secret Wars of the CIA* (New York: Simon and Schuster, 1987).

Wroe, Ann, *Lives, Lies and the Iran–Contra Affair* (London, I. B. Tauris and Co. Ltd, 1991).

Whitewater

Bartley, Robert L. (ed.), *Whitewater* (New York: Dow Jones and Co. Inc., 1994).

Bartley, Robert L. (ed.), *Whitewater*, vol. 2 (New York: Dow Jones and Co. Inc., 1997).

Brummett, John, *Highwire* (New York: Hyperion, 1994).

Drew, Elizabeth, *On the Edge: The Clinton Presidency* (New York: Simon and Schuster, 1994).

Falconer, Peter, 'Whitewater, Partisanship and U.S. Congressional Oversight', *Talking Politics*, September 1995, pp. 53–8.

Gerth, Jeff, 'Clintons Joined S & L Operator in an Ozark Real-Estate Venture', *New York Times*, 8 March 1992.

Stewart, James B., *Blood Sport: The President and His Adversaries* (New York: Simon and Schuster, 1996).

US Senate, *The Special Committee's Whitewater Report* (Washington, DC: Government Printing Office, 1996).

Walden, Gregory S., *On Best Behaviour: The Clinton Administration and Ethics in Government* (Indianapolis: Hudson Institute, 1996).

Whitewater Internet Sources

Arkansas Times: local coverage of Whitewater:
   http://www.arktimes.com/news.htm

Court TV: web site – cases and hearings:
   http://www.courttv.com/library/government/whitewater/

Washington Post: chronology of Whitewater:
   http://www.washingtonpost.com/wp-stv/national/longterm/wwtr/chron.htm

Congress

Adams, James Ring, *The Big Fix: Inside the S & L Scandal* (New York: John Wiley, 1990).

Banducci, Susan A. and Karp, Jeffrey A., 'Electoral Consequences of Scandal and Reapportionment in the 1992 House Elections', *American Politics Quarterly*, vol. 22, January 1994, pp. 3–26.

Barry, John M., *The Ambition and the Power* (New York: Viking, 1989).

Congressional Quarterly, *Congressional Ethics: History, Facts and Controversy* (Washington, 1992).

Jacobson Gary C. and Dimock, Michael A., 'Checking Out: The Effects of Bank Overdrafts on the 1992 Elections', *American Journal of Political Science*, vol. 38, August 1994, pp. 601–24.

Jennings, Bruce and Callahan, Daniel (eds), *Representation and Responsibility: Exploring Legislative Ethics* (New York: Plenum Press, 1985).

Lowenstein, Daniel Hays, 'On Campaign Finance Reform: The Root of All Evil Is Deeply Rooted', *Hofstra Law Review*, vol. 18, Fall 1989, pp. 301–35.

Mann, Thomas E. and Ornstein, Norman J. (eds), *Congress, the Press, and the Public* (Washington, Brookings and AEI, 1994).

Patterson, Samuel C. and Caldwell, Gregory A., 'Standing Up for Congress: Variations in Public Esteem since the 1960s', *Legislative Studies Quarterly*, vol. 15, February 1990, pp. 25–47.

Rozell, Mark J., *In Contempt of Congress: Postwar Press Coverage on Capitol Hill* (New York, Praeger, 1996).

Sorauf, Frank J., *Inside Campaign Finance: Myths and Realities* (New Haven: Yale University Press, 1992).

Thompson, Dennis F., 'Mediated Corruption: The Case of the Keating Five', *American Political Science Review*, vol. 87, No. 2, June 1993, pp. 369–81.

Thompson, Dennis F., *Ethics in Congress: From Individual to Institutional Corruption* (Washington, DC: The Brookings Institution, 1995).

Uslaner, Eric M., *The Decline of Comity in Congress* (University of Michigan Press, 1993).

Index